PENGUIN BOOKS

FIELDS OF FRIENDLY STRIFE

John Janovy, Jr., a professor of biology at the University of Nebraska, is the author of several highly praised science/natural history books, *Keith County Journal*, *Yellowlegs*, and *Back in Keith County*. He lives with his family in Lincoln, Nebraska.

John Janovy, Jr.

Fields of Friendly Strife

PENGUIN BOOKS

PENGUIN BOOKS
Published by the Penguin Group
Viking Penguin Inc., 40 West 23rd Street,
New York, New York 10010, U.S.A.
Penguin Books Ltd, 27 Wrights Lane, London W8 5TZ, England
Penguin Books Australia Ltd, Ringwood, Victoria, Australia
Penguin Books Canada Limited, 2801 John Street,
Markham, Ontario, Canada L3R 1B4
Penguin Books (N.Z.) Ltd, 182–190 Wairau Road,
Auckland 10, New Zealand

Penguin Books Ltd, Registered Offices: Harmondsworth,
Middlesex, England

First published in the United States of America by
Viking Penguin Inc., 1987
Published in Penguin Books 1988

Grateful acknowledgment is made for permission to
reprint the following material:

Excerpts from *Sports Illustrated Volleyball*. © 1972 Time Inc.
Published by Harper & Row, Publishers, Inc.
Reprinted by permission of Sports Illustrated.

Douglas MacArthur quotation on page 69. Used by permission of
the United States Military Academy.

LIBRARY OF CONGRESS CATALOGING IN PUBLICATION DATA
Janovy, John.
Fields of friendly strife / John Janovy, Jr.
p.   cm.
Reprint. Originally published: New York, N.Y., U.S.A.: Viking,
1987.
ISBN 0 14 00.9373 7
1. Janovy, Jena.   2. Athletes—United States—Biography.
3. Athletics—Psychological aspects.   4. Fathers and daughters—
United States—Case studies.   I. Title.
[GV697.J34J36   1988]
796'.092'4—dc19
[B]   87-29190

Printed in the United States of America by
R. R. Donnelley & Sons Company, Harrisonburg, Virginia
Set in Linotron Aster

You have to hate to lose so much
That you want to win so much
That you'll work so hard
That you'll never lose again.

Foreword

This has been an exceedingly difficult writing assignment and I'll tell you why. First, the book is about my family, one daughter in particular, and when a person writes about his immediate family readers tend to be somewhat put off unless the story falls into one of several genres: children writing about celebrity parents, parents writing about childhood tragedy, or that of Erma Bombeck. This book is not in any of these categories. Second, the book deals with sports, and people tend to take sports either too seriously or not seriously enough. I'll come back to this point later. Third, although competition has a number of characteristics which everyone recognizes (victory, loss, effort, injury), it also has some other features which are not so widely understood, or even noticed. These are what this book is about. For example, we respond emotionally, either as a participant or a fan, to structure brought about by timing and pace, regardless of the outcome of events. Compare the flow of action in baseball with that in basketball and you'll see what I mean. In one or two places I've tried to match the structure of sentences and paragraphs with the timing of a game. Some readers might find it hard to get through a chapter that's written like a volleyball match. Others can probably handle this challenge easily. These comments are no reflection on respective mental abilities, but only say what we all know, namely, that different people have different expectations of the printed page—or of volleyball. Finally, most of us get our sports information from newspapers, magazines, and radio or television. As a result, our picture of athletics is often molded by the media. In sports journalism it is common practice to write about men, winners and scores, the immediacy of bench-clearing brawls, league standings, contract disputes, drug problems, and legal battles. This book does not deal much with these things. *Fields of Friendly Strife* is not sports journalism.

The research for this small volume took about ten or twelve years, from around the time one of our children started in organized athletics until her freshman year in college. The study consisted mainly of watching ball games, parents, players, coaches, and fans; analyzing the architecture of gyms and courts during time-outs; driving and listening to kids talk about playing ball; and taking pictures. From these experiences I feel as if I can state unequivocally that athletic competition is an ingrained part of human biology. It would be interesting some day to explore the evolutionary origins of athletics, to try to discover what role sport plays in a primal society, and perhaps even to perform an experiment to find out what would happen if a group of humans were to be deprived of all contests. This book addresses these scholarly problems in only a casual manner. Instead, it's mostly an attempt to answer in retrospect a much more personal question: Why is our little girl playing ball?

The writing was also exceedingly difficult because I tried to satisfy a large number of people who read the manuscript and provided strong, often negative, comments about some of my favorite parts (which I then removed). In the process I discovered that there are not very many whose view of athletics falls somewhere between the two extremes of those who take sport too seriously and those who don't take it seriously enough. If you are among the former, my words may seem too philosophical because you believe that victory is an end unto itself, and the struggle an all-consuming personal allegory that ends at the scoreboard. If you are among the latter, your failure to look beyond the arena may block your efforts to determine the ultimate value of what on the surface looks like play. Translated, these statements mean it would be much easier to write a book about girls playing ball if most people honestly felt, or at least acted as if they felt, that there might be more to a game than the winner and the score.

Finally, I would like to thank all those who helped with the writing, either directly or indirectly. I am very grateful to the coaches who are not only mentioned in various places throughout the text—Larry Fuerst, Myron Oehlerking, and John Strain—but also read the manuscript and passed along their comments and advice. All those associated with the women's basketball program at the University of Nebraska-Omaha, especially Lady Mavericks' coach Cherri Mankenberg, assistant Linda Mills, and women's athletic coordinator Connie Claussen, provided material and depth, perhaps without realizing it. And, of course, Jena herself was patient with questions from a parent who seemed, at times, to be shockingly ignorant of games he'd watched for years.

Others who helped at least indirectly are parents, children, booksellers, family members, friends, students, in fact almost anyone who expressed an interest in the manuscript once they heard I was working on it. I discovered from their reactions that opinions on athletics are stronger than those on sex, money, war, pollution, and politics. This is not an unkind comment, but instead my expression of wonder. I simply had no idea how strongly others felt about sport until I started writing on the subject. Why did I begin this project? Because a few years ago it became obvious that my wife, Karen, had given birth to a reasonably gifted athlete and as time went by I found myself thinking more and more about some words, almost poetry, that I'd read as a college student. The quote began "Upon the fields of friendly strife . . . " After a decade of thinking about the message, I concluded that I'd discovered, after all, just what there was to be found on those fields.

John Janovy, Jr.
Lincoln, Nebraska
May 1985

Contents

Fields of
Friendly
Strife

1

Fifteen Years

*O*ne of our children asked me the other day "has your marriage been a happy one?" The question was followed by a lament often expressed by those in their early twenties, suddenly alone with their emotions and the remnants of a recent relationship, namely that "things never seem to work out." I mumbled an answer that must have come more from history than from fairy tales—somehow that word "happy" wasn't quite adequate to describe the last twenty-four years. Relationships are not necessarily happy or unhappy, instead they are an avenue upon which one can explore some of the richness of the human experience on earth. Our social interactions are productive, exciting, trying; they bring out the best, and sometimes the worst, of what we have to offer ourselves and others. In this sense, relationships, even marriages, must be in the same category as art, music, literature, architecture, war, and sport.

The next day, because of a rare combination of events, all three children found themselves together posing by the fireplace for a picture. My wife, Karen, aimed the camera while I sat consumed with the sheer wonder at what we'd foisted off on the world, thinking back to when the kids were born, trying to reconstruct the expectations that we'd had so many years ago, suddenly astonished by the way they'd grown tall, at least in the case of two of them, and surprisingly urbane, in the case of the third. Later, talking family small talk after a Sunday dinner, we fell to reminiscing, and the oldest one, remembering some pictures she must have seen around the house in years past, asked if we could show home movies. There is, of course, no need to describe these 8mm films except to say that everything derogatory, all of it together, that you've ever read, or heard, about home movies falls far short of expressing their low quality. They did, however, show the kids playing ball.

I found myself studying a few particular shots with unusual interest, wondering if I'd had some subconscious premonition that I would want, fifteen years later, a record of children playing with a toy football. In the darkened living room the fluttering out-of-focus images, smeared in places with the total white of a lens pointed accidentally toward the sun, showed two small children. They were about four, maybe five. One hiked the ball to the other then ran out for a pass. They traded places. I put the projector into reverse and went back over the scene, this time studying the throwing motion carefully. One tried a punt and the ball went straight up in the air. Then they each took turns running, ball cradled, cutting back against the grain, dodging imagined tacklers. Everyone in the room knew why all this action seemed so interesting fifteen years later. One of the kids, a special friend and neighbor, had moved far away. The last we'd heard, he'd been offered a scholarship to play ball in college. The other kid sat in our living room, her eyes bright in the darkness. She too goes to college on a scholarship—to play ball.

In between the day the films were taken and the recent Sunday screening were all the decisions, events, wins, and losses that would forever be a part of our lives. Not once during those years had anyone said "this is an important time for us," but values, traditions, and various ways to deal with adversity were all learned, or at least experienced, sometimes tried, never to be forgotten. Home movies, the most amateurish of media, revealed a fundamental rule of life. When it comes to raising children, we're all amateurs. I see now, hidden in a tiny strip of film, the way we answered a question that every young couple must face: What do I do now? I don't know what other parents did in order to while away the time between meals and stories. To one of ours, the oldest, we gave books; at first she ate them, but twenty-three years later decided to write them. To the youngest, we gave cars; at first he buried them in the garden, but sixteen years later decided to drive them. And to the middle child, we threw a ball.

This child, however, was a girl. That fact alone meant that games had to have certain outcomes. There would be the inevitable conflict with dancing; would we finally admit that what is done upon a floor with lines might also be ballet? Days do not contain enough hours for both piano and basketball; could we come to accept the idea that a screaming crowd makes another kind of music? At times exhaustion ruled over homework; would the things a girl could do with her body always take precedence over things she could do with her brain, or would athletics be shown, eventually, to be very much a matter of the mind? Games have an unquestioned immediacy—a task, an accomplishment, a victory, or loss; no one need wait the infinite years to adulthood to find out if a launched sphere will in fact pass through a metal ring. This is not so with the more scholarly pursuits. We assume, never question, that a quarter of a century down the road, literature and math will give us powers over emptiness. But will sport? And for a girl?

On the surface, yes: You can always jog, swim, play golf,

racquetball, coach, keep in shape, be proud of the way you look and feel, teach others to do the same. But let us be honest. When matched against architecture, running five miles a day is the most trivial of human endeavors; compared to a Thomas Pynchon novel, swimming laps is mindless at best; and, beside a scientist's decision to help build a nuclear weapon, the coach's choice of players is a flashing event we raise to importance only by our endless discussion of it.

In the fifteen years since two four-year-olds played ball for the movies, my nation has walked upon the moon, lost a war, dabbled in some others, sent a desperate message of deteriorating earth on a journey into space beyond the planets, and made a mockery of the sacred distinction between species by mixing their genes in the lab. While all this was happening, Karen and I bought a store full of shoes, uniforms, basketballs, footballs, soccer balls, baseballs; molded our rear ends to every barren bleacher seat in everything anybody ever called a gym; insulted every official in a several-state region; evaluated every coach who dared try to build a team out of a motley crew of kids; wore out several cars; listened to a lifetime's supply of teenie-bopper music; sat night after night in motel bars rehashing plays with team parents; laughed, cried, searched the sports pages of local newspapers; took pictures; and raised money. At the end, watching films on a Sunday afternoon, trying to imagine what hopes, dreams, and feelings were in the minds of three children, I couldn't help but wonder if the world was really a better place for our having done the thing we'd done.

A question of this sort, posed to oneself, demands that apparently mundane acts be put into some kind of a broader perspective. Our attempt to do just that may have brought us to a realization of the value of sport. As for athletics, two of our three children, the tall and strapping ones, discovered early on that it takes a certain dedication to physical punishment, often inflicted upon yourself, to play seriously at games. This is not to say they shied away entirely, but rather to suggest that perspective comes at different times to each of us and may take many forms. They were eventually able to stand with a book in one hand and a ball in the other and make a rational choice about which to use for what purpose. No such enlightenment intruded upon the halcyon days of our younger daughter. If, standing holding the book and ball, she'd been asked for what they were to be used, she'd have questioned your sanity, tossed the book on the nearest table, and thrown you the ball—hard.

Games inexorably lead a child down certain paths. Parents follow for various reasons, few of which they can explain, least of all to themselves. In the end, it is only fair for them, and their children, to ask: Of what value is this activity upon which I've spent so much time and effort, but which seems to offer so little in the way of an ultimate payoff? The pages that follow contain my attempt to answer this question. After having tried to come to terms with organized athletics, I'm convinced that sport is not worthless, meaningless, mere entertainment, a means to quick riches for the specially endowed, or a measure of the national vigor. I'm also convinced that there's more to it than implied by the maudlin, hackneyed phrase "building character."

Humans may indeed have a genetic predisposition for play that ritualizes a fantasy of our own primeval state. If so, then we have carried that trait through our history and into the nuclear age. We picture ourselves, 30,000 years ago, as unkempt and tribal, locked in a constant struggle against nature and disease. We must have placed a premium on strength and speed, we think, on quickness, agility—characte᛫ ᛫ tics we now associate with successful athletes. But we also tend to associate these skills with the male. It takes a runner to chase down the mammoth, a weight lifter to carry the haunches back to camp. Rough games of men and boys had to be training for these life roles. But it takes only nimble fingers for the mates to gather berries.

The trouble with fantasies is that they rarely survive close scrutiny in strong light. Training for life roles that no longer exist doesn't adequately explain why this little girl is playing ball. Maybe she is in training for roles that exist but remain unacknowledged by the bleachers full of rowdy fans, or maybe don't exist, but remain for her to forge from experience. In both cases, the fantasy is incomplete, inadequate, or inapplicable to modern times. I reject the latter; anything as deeply embedded in our psyche as athletics must surely merit exploration for its own sake with no preconceived notions about its immediacy, or lack thereof. These are heavy issues to bring forth from childhood games. Perhaps in this attempt to discover the value of sport in such a case, I should return to the beginning, to the first indication that an athlete had been born.

2

Indications

*H*er older sister was a mouthy sort, given to literature and the arts. There was little love lost between them; that's how sisters are sometimes, at least in their early years. The older one showed signs she would be fluent verbally: Her first intelligible speech consisted of two words. Later she wrote scathing commentary in the high school newspaper and got blackballed from the National Honor Society because of it. She seemed to spend a lot of time in trouble, in her room, and in her car. The younger one, at age thirteen, however, was all happiness and light, cooperative, with swarms of friends. The older one looked out a window one day at a crowd of children playing, and summarized her younger sister's inclinations, again, in two words: pro jock. Then the younger one threw a baseball the length of the yard, across the street, and into the neighbor's garage. A year later she did the same thing with a basketball.

She was sick as a very young child, with colds upon colds, fevers, and a particularly severe case of the chicken pox. She was given the usual round of toys, most of them hand-me-downs. Then the details get fuzzy. Karen made some dresses, girls' shades of pink, yellow, or light blue to match her eyes. A photographer posed her sitting on a tiny chair with her legs crossed, in white tights and matching filamentous cascades of hair. A block of time seems to be missing. The next image is only a memory, but it comes from a pitcher's mound distorted by heat waves through which gaping boys tug at their caps and twist gloves too big for eleven-year-old fingers. Her right hand is down across her left ankle, her right leg kicks behind in total concentration, a rock hard baseball ricochets off a backstop, a wiry umpire bawls "steee-rike!" and a couple of ruffians yell "blow it past them gravy suckin' pigs!" while the thunderheads begin to gather and city park lights come on in that country where Pat Jordan began to fail as a major league ballplayer.

At times like these, when one sets about to examine the reasons for playing at games, the search often begins for the first recognition that an athlete has been born. Twenty years gone to business, and now things are like they are and she is like she is but we don't remember how or when it came about. Did we roll a ball on the floor when she was a year old? I think we did that with all our kids. We must have rolled the ball off to the left, off to the right, faster and faster maybe, doing nothing but entertaining ourselves and testing the physical limits of a toddler because she laughed when we did it. Was it that little laughter we wanted more of when we threw something up for her to catch, all before she could talk very well? Yes, it must have been.

The house is no longer filled with children's laughter. But from the stands we can still see a smile. She's forced a turnover, broken the other guard's rhythm, or concentration, and suddenly the ball is lost. In a flurry of arms somebody forgets to dribble, a whistle cuts the yelling, and the opposing coach rises from the bench. But a man in a striped shirt points to a spot on the floor in front of that coach. She never looks at the bench or into the stands. She takes her place out of bounds and is handed the ball. She flicks it in then gets it back. Somewhere behind those blue eyes an analysis of impending motion is converted into a plan of action that once again explodes. Her opponents press, meet her beneath her own basket, try to trap at midcourt. She goes around. Some people are fighting, jumping. Then there is a score. She steals the other team's inbound pass. This goes on and on. Periodically she smiles and high school girls high-five it. We watch from the top row of seats and wonder if that smile is what is left of the little child laughter we used to get when we rolled a ball on the floor. Her uniform is white and blue; the other team's are red. Red knows it better not roll the ball on the floor because she will chase it. We could have told them that from the stands, from those hazy memories. Red rolls the ball on the floor anyway. Now she not only chases it, she gets it. We could have told them that, too, from those same memories.

We see in retrospect there were indications she would be "coachable." That willingness to cooperate, try almost any kind of play, happily, were subtle manifestations, showing as if through some screen, things whose true significance we didn't know at the time. The articulation of this trait is essential to the understanding of a potential athlete. There are those who control their bodies, those who control their minds and those who do both. Then there are driven, individualistic types who have no control whatsoever over their runaway desires to build an image of ideas, synthesize myths, and express feelings. This last type will never be an athlete, especially a team athlete. Instead, he or she will be the artist. But those who have control over themselves are not threatened by observations of their performances. They see throughout the world a bountiful harvest of techniques, opportunities, possibilities. Their self-confidence smooths over the natural affront which comes to most of us with criticism. If they are truly secure, they take a criticism, somebody else's idea, in good grace, try it, and if it works, add it to their repertoire. After all, there may come a time when another's idea will work. If it comes down to a question of playing or not playing, one never throws out anything. Speed, deceptiveness, the ability to control a sphere, these are the skills that make up for lack of inches. One gets into a game by whatever means that seem necessary. People who do that are likely to be coachable.

There were indications she would be small. We called her "Peanut" within a week after she came to live at our house. We still call her "Peanut" sometimes, along with other diminutive names. When you're very young, small is "cute." Inches are added and measured as you stand straight against the doorjamb and the dated marks that bring back memories are drawn there for mothers to study in their quiet times, remembering "when she was this tall." Then comes a year when the distance between the lines is not so far, and another when there is no distance at all. Talk turns from "she's growing" to "sometimes kids have a late growing spurt, even in high school." The late spurt never arrived. The final admission she'd be small came during the annual purchase of shoes. "Basketball?" said the salesman, laying boxes out on the floor. "Usually girls have about all the height they're going to get at your age." I put my hand over my face. The salesman was very sympathetic over the facts her feet had revealed. She smiled and nodded in a sort of resigned way. We know that resigned, controlled, good-natured nod to an affront; it's the same one we see when she gets called for a foul. Behind the acceptance is an "in your face, turkey!"

There were early indications she'd stand out among people doing exercises. Dance recital show-off evening is of more significance than one realizes at first, when a group of small girls lines up on the stage. Psychological ropes of thick, pure emotion tie each of them to a mother in the audience, a mother who made the costume, sewed on every sequin that now reflects the colored lights. But these children are alone at last in front of the judging world. Some handle their feet well. Others are overwhelmed by the audience and just stand there. Some try very hard to see beyond the footlights to where grandparents are sitting. Others miss a beat and are out of step, and some always follow the missed step. It's the most heart-jerking spectacle civilized society is able to put together. But one of them never misses a beat or looks out into the audience or follows or just stands there. She may not have the absolute grace by which even a small town knows a world class ballerina has been born, but she has control, precision, coordination, and most of all, peripheral vision. She knows exactly where she is and where she is supposed to be in the next few seconds—a sense of place in a rapidly shifting scene of many characters. Years later, on another kind of stage, she will also be singled out for her movements and court sense—elbowed, tripped, fouled, held, double-teamed, pushed into a bench, and hated, this last by a father whose daughter can't seem to get the ball out of the backcourt when Peanut plays guard in the City League.

Finally, there were indications she would play at top speed. One year a man declared his intent to jump over the Snake River Canyon on a motorcycle. Someone called it "sports" and decided to cover the event on television. Boys set up ramps of bricks and boards on sidewalks all over the country. Her town was no different—the ramp appeared out by the mailbox and neighborhood boys backed off a few yards and ran their bicycles over it. She watched for a while, went into the garage, then came around the corner on her bike. No parent likes this kind of play, especially if a child has permanent teeth. But the ramp, and the speeds, were low. She disappeared down the block. We were relieved; there must have been some other business on her mind. When she reappeared in the distance it was at whatever maximum velocity bicycles would go in those days. A certain fascination with mortal danger halts even parents in their tracks. I can still remember the sound of her bicycle hitting a ramp of bricks and boards. But once was enough; she'd almost lost it, her front wheel turning sideways in midair. The boys went back to playing ball.

The decision to back away a full block, however, is worthy of exploration. Why had some decided fifty feet was enough and why did she think that fifty feet was nowhere near enough? Because she knew even then she couldn't get a bike to top speed in less than a block. One doesn't enter competition at less than top speed. Had the neighbor boys not realized it was competition? Without a full block you never see your best. She gives herself no choice but to see her best. Driving oneself to top speed is an act of brazenness in the face of possible failure. But then she doesn't fail that often. Maybe the times she's failed have been those times she hasn't put her own unique combination of talents to the task, or when success has been defined by someone else. A personal definition of success must be in the subconscious of every kid who takes a ball in hand, or puts on a pair of spikes, or stands at the end of a black line down the bottom of some pool. Maybe some surrogate redefinition of success is what every fan hopes to get with the price of a ticket.

Those are interesting maybes. Among them could be the answer to why she is now in her pregame ritual: In the wing position to the side of the free-throw circle, she faces away from the basket, twirls the ball to bounce on the floor at her feet, catches it on the bounce, turns and fires. She does this over and over again. Then she moves to the other side. Then she adds a fake. She never misses. She'll miss in the game, but not now. So it's finally come down to basketball, has it, that incredibly complex sport of sports with its motion and its giants? There's glory in basketball, but there's more: Complexity makes any game vulnerable to innovation; when decisions must be made at breakneck speed, the quick and the disciplined have an advantage. If there is a ball, then it is to be possessed. If there are teammates, then they are to be clear for the shot. If there are opponents who have no control over your thoughts, have no idea about your plans for the next second, they can be denied both the ball and the shot. These are her definitions of success, her own terms. And when the game starts, she will see if the definitions fly.

3

The White
Football

*T*he football is a miniature, about eight inches long, rubber, but inflatable. It fit her tiny hands so many years ago. Some families would treat it as a relic: She learned to play ball with that particular white football. No one seems to know where it came from. It's of exceptionally high quality for a toy, so it must be old. We feared it lost once and searched the stores for an equivalent. They don't exist. Then we found it when the snow melted in March. It's made of heavy rubber with raised fake laces and, at least when we first got it, was perfectly proportioned. The pigskin texture was even molded into the rubber. Today it's worn smooth.

Now we get into the depths of ignorance and wisdom that come only from experience. There are literally thousands of young boys playing organized football in this country. Additional thousands, if not tens of thousands, play high school "ball" and thousands more play at colleges, junior colleges, and universities. Then there are the professionals, not only the real professionals, but also a goodly number of scrubbier minor league pro teams. Add to these the Canadians—but they use a different ball. Supporting this enormous population of football players is another sizable population of coaches. The coaches are the tip of an iceberg of former football players who must number in the hundreds of thousands. Any of these people could tell you with authority how to throw a football. But I do not belong to any of the above groups, so when I tell you that throwing a football is a more difficult task than throwing round balls, there is an untainted original observation behind that statement. I know, baseball players will tell you about curves, sinkers, control; but those are things a person learns in addition to throwing a ball well. A spiral, however, is a very basic element of a thrown football, and throwing a spiral requires a combination of arm and hand/finger motions that can be a true test for a child.

"Keep your wrist straight, your fingers on top of the ball, your elbow under the ball, your thumb and first finger about here on this black circle around one end, and aim the other end at the place you want it to go." I must have read those instructions on the back of a cereal box. They may not be correct. It didn't matter.

"All right, Daddy!" Six-year-old girls are the sweetest things, especially when they launch a spiral.

"Run out for a pass."

"Yes, Daddy!" I don't remember how far I threw the white football, or whether she caught it, only that "run out for a pass" was part of her working language at the time. It would be an interesting study of American culture to determine just how early in life children can routinely execute the wide receiver movements that accompany the command.

At some point in the few years after all this began, white football became a serious test of limits. I would stand on the front porch in the evenings and throw the thing as hard as I could, with her on a dead run about fifteen feet away. If she didn't catch it, the white football would go down the storm sewer. When that got boring, there were the distance contests, then burnout, each of us trying to throw the ball so hard the other couldn't, or wouldn't try to, catch it. The rules were simple: You got a point when the other person missed. You could play to ten, fifty, a hundred, or infinity, as long as the evening supplied the light. By the time she was twelve, she was winning regularly at burnout. By the time she was fourteen, she could win at burnout with a real football. Baseballs had been taken away from her. They were dangerous weapons.

"Now watch the ball all the way into your hands. Watch it as you catch it."

"Okay, Daddy, throw it!" Kids are so neat when their eyes get great big over some excitement they know is on the way. The white football never has a chance. Blue eyes track. Hands catch. The trapped ball is tucked away and with a sudden accelerating burst the wide receiver breaks free, her deceptively random cuts and hesitations working their way toward an imaginary goal line. She's been watching too much television.

Before long, brother is old enough to participate. Now backyard white football becomes a matter of teaching and macho: How to use her skills to teach him without subjecting him to the continuous punishment of being beaten by a girl. If she weren't his sister, you could get by with letting him get beaten time and again until he either learned pass defense, or learned to run the wide receiver patterns, or quit. The solution, when it comes, is easy. When he gets too frustrated, then he gets to be the quarterback, she the wide receiver, and poor old dad the cornerback. The cornerback is patient. He knows if he defends successfully one time in five, it will stir the fires of friendly strife, in her. He knows a few minutes of throwing to her will once again build the sweet feeling of greatness in the boy. She never misses, even the unreasonable ones. She's watched too many oblong objects struggle through the prairie skies to miss a ball thrown by a brother. The psychology of backyard NFL evens itself out. We return to lessons: son plays cornerback, daughter wide receiver; son plays wide receiver, daughter cornerback. They are difficult lessons indeed, just as difficult as piano.

Then one year he beats her once in ten. He's grown; she's stopped. If she can be beaten once in ten, can the world be challenged, the space invasion repelled? Yes. It's such a natural and routine thing, backyard NFL, but it has laid to rest a myth that you have to reach the higher atmosphere of glory sport before the lessons of athletics begin to seep into your intellectual life. Nothing could be further from the truth than such myths. The lessons are there in the yard ready to be grasped by anyone. A younger brother has defined success, for the moment, in terms of his sister's ability to catch, or prevent him from catching, a tiny white football. Finally one year he defines success in terms of his own ability to catch, or defend, against her. She is no longer superhuman, but there will never be a time when he doubts that a girl can play ball.

How can anyone who doesn't believe this kind of sport is true education send a child to school to learn to read, then expect that child to be able to read outside of class? Our species has an incredible ability to turn the "trivial" into something of value. Those who focus only on the trivial never seem to understand, and perhaps are incapable of using, this ability. Only the setting—the backyard—is trivial, and success there is the first step on the road to ever-lasting achievements. In the yard you can get that first taste of accomplishment against odds with your body and a white football. But if it's to mean anything, it has to stick in your mind.

"I beat Jena today on that one throw," he says, then adds, "I came back and she got beat."

"You ran a good pattern, turned her around." It's evening, after dinner. He's resisting the piano and lingering over the comics. She's been sent to practice first. That's also a small victory for him. I am sitting with the other half of the paper, hiding a smile; the subtleties of human behavior are a constant amazement. Whoever resists going to the piano the longest has defeated the system by which parents provide their kids with "culture." After dinner, I can get very philosophical about the ways humans, even my own children, express their wins and losses. It is crazy to think this way, but I find myself wondering if he'd been made to practice first, if that would have somehow invalidated his one catch against a sister cornerback. Does a victory, no matter how small, have to be followed by another before it is admitted into the permanence of self-confidence? In this tense atmosphere no one dares comment on what comes out of the piano. Too much praise for her music and there might appear without warning another "backyard" upon which she, his most immediate symbol of a competitive world, cannot be beaten, at least yet. So Karen and I both keep our mouths shut and listen. These are notes never to be forgotten.

"You did pretty well, John," she says without missing a chord or turning her head. She never mentions the dozens of times she slapped the ball away, or picked it out of his hands and ran it all the way back, or the times she stood alone in the end zone between the apple trees while dad threw the white football into the branches. But she knows. She also knows he'll go out again tomorrow convinced he can beat her on every throw. If he manages twice instead of once, she'll keep quiet again. This is not the real NFL after all—no one's livelihood, no one's future, depends on victory. Who are we kidding? Someone's future may depend more on beating a girl cornerback in the yard than it ever would in those higher leagues. And she's learned he needs success as badly as she did at half his age.

She's grown now, into a teen-age woman. She has things to do, places to go, after school. He's busy with his friends, his own version of NFL down the block, his cities and highways in his room, his analysis of ancient movies on television. My profession has turned busy; it's out of town, late, almost to dark, an evening obligation. Backyard NFL suffers. We think we've outgrown it, that what we're doing instead is an advancement up some arbitrary scale. There are times when you can look around at your life and ask what it is that suddenly makes you feel times have changed; that a door has been slammed shut behind, never to open again. In this case it's the end of backyard white football, no longer the evening ritual with priority over all else. Maybe it began to end when the danger of an ankle twisted in fun was no longer a risk worth taking. Maybe it started to end when lessons stuck, when it became obvious that she was a superb ball handler and we knew the white football had done its task.

We accept those maybes. The white football is there on the floor as I take out the garbage on my way to work, pre-dawn. I smile. Some day, worn buddy, when the old man needs a redefinition of success, a kid will pick you up and say "run out for some passes, Daddy!"

4

Game Films

*T*he room is very large, dark, and there are two hundred people out there somewhere—my students. I am a biology teacher by profession and the lesson for today concerns the most complex species of all, the human. We are watching what I have come to call "game films." Margaret Mead is on the screen. The camera pans the New Guinea highlands. Near-naked men jabber, knotted hair, smeared with pork grease, curling down over their eyes; children move quickly between the men's legs; women gaggle, their breasts hanging, heads held high and proud. Their postures are taunting. The very lilt of their skittering speech is taunting. In the distance are tiered farms, mist. The incredible greens of the New Guinea mountains are faded now; the film is old.

"These are the Dani," says Margaret Mead, "and their environment is war."

A man half-heartedly chunks mucky soil with a primitive wooden hoe. His mind is not on his business. His eyes flicker toward the hills. The camera moves slowly, almost thoughtfully, over the village. Skin glistens. Children throw spears made of grass blades. One, who cannot be more than two or three years old, gets it right in the rear end and stands bawling while the older ones taunt and throw more grass blades. Few connect; even at this age they dodge quickly. The movements are the same ones used by their fathers to dodge arrows fired at a hundred feet. The play spear fights are early training for serious grown-up business that defines a culture, claims Margaret Mead. My students' faces are barely visible in the screen's reflected light; I wonder how each of them, sitting quietly a universe away from New Guinea, is translating the Dani experience into meaning. The camera closes in on a warrior. He turns, looks directly at the freshman biology class. Smoke on the horizon behind him signals a skirmish. The warrior smiles. I've seen that smile before, I think. Oh, now I remember. Jena has a game tonight.

Our brains allow strange associations—a Dani man gazes at my class, as he's done every semester for years, smiling at the call to war, and my thoughts turn to a high school girl anticipating, as she must be this very moment, the whistles, buzzers, shouting, ritual music, school cheers, of her own battles and, just as inevitably as in the New Guinea highlands, injuries. But it was the smile that caused the two images to surface together in my thoughts. Some indescribable feature of a grin, captured decades ago on a face probably now long gone into eternity, brings to mind a basketball game to be played in the future. I suppose both the warrior's and the girl's smile could be measured, characterized in a scientific way anthropologists might have for classifying facial expressions. No parent who's watched a kid chase a ball since before she was able to walk, however, needs science to explain the association. Both the man and the girl await the game. While hers is basketball and his is played with arrows and spears, the anticipation of a contest brings the same look to both faces. Stakes are different, we assume. But to the Dani, whatever the stakes that lie beyond the costs of conflict, they are simply the currency it takes to play at the life games that define their culture. And if asked to analyze her sport in academic terms, sitting there in the locker room getting her ankles wrapped, so too would say Jena, with a smile.

Film brings to us a vision that is beyond the picture. We are given the opportunity to see an exact and unique moment in history repeated over and over so long as we are willing to manipulate the projector. The act of smiling at war can be isolated, run again and again, forward and reverse, and every time fires are set on the horizon and just as predictably a warrior smiles at the knowledge he will soon be in a fight, and a parent is reminded of a game. We can also, at will, simply by controlling a machine's switch, provide the unique event with a context. Run the film backward far enough, and Margaret Mead will explain what you are about to see; run it forward far enough, and you'll be shown how war is integrated into the larger social structure by which the Dani have made peace with their tropical island. But no such time machine exists for one girl smiling at the thought of games. There is no button we can push to isolate her instants for analysis, no anthropologist available at our fingertips to provide the context, to select scenes that integrate her pounding dribble into American society. I suppose it was for this last reason, having seen what "game films" could do for students watching primal spear fights, that I decided to take some pictures of Jena playing ball.

Which means, of course, that I joined the ranks of the world's sports photographers. One has plenty of company here; no single human activity is photographed in this country to the extent that athletic competition is. Not surprisingly, sports photography has spawned a wealth of creative talent behind the camera. Artists' drives to capture the essence of sport have built an archive of technical history: uniforms, equipment, plays, fields and gymnasiums, the technical history of photography itself, are all implied in what is captured on film. Videotape adds a skip step to this evolution of our culture. We can now see instantly the facts behind the impression, things never imagined, still not believed, like the midair movements of black giants. Someone lifts into air at the top of the key, floats toward a backboard, arms go one way, body and head another, the giant is still in the air, arm stretches, ball rolls off fingers, goes up and around a clawing mass of hands, then into the basket. Bodies crash into cheerleaders. It's called a layup. Twelve-year-old boys try these movements in a thousand cities.

Humans are notorious imitators; we cannot deny this fundamental character. No matter what the activity, movements achieving success will quickly be taken up by others. But first, you have to see what is happening. For example, Frederic Remington, working with watercolors before the time of movies, captured horses' legs in midair at full gallop, lariats and rifles flying through the dusty sunsets of the American West. He is set apart not only by his skill with paint, but also, perhaps even more, by his vision. Remington actually saw what so many other artists could not—the movements of horses suspended at top speed.

The unique workings of an artist's nervous system have now been reconstructed, at least in part, on printed circuits. A young person sits in front of a television set. The galloping giants are now in the NBA and their moves are explained by an expert in instant replay slow motion: Dribble at rocket speed, then slow, suddenly accelerate, switch hands, squirt past the defending guard, leap, head fake, switch hands again, double-pump, basket, foul, hit the floor; three-point play coming up. The kid turns off the set, picks up a basketball and heads out to the driveway to try these same movements. A player has just been shown that perceived limits to the human's abilities are only that: perceived, not real. Now begins the self-discipline required to introduce some of the NBA into a schoolyard. It is in this sense that sports photography changes the way a game is played.

In the above example, "I see" became "I understand." The child with a ball may not have understood what was required to actually perform the movements shown on TV, but nevertheless realized that success couldn't be achieved sitting in front of the screen. The televised slam dunk is what an anthropologist would call a "cultural item" no less infectious for a segment of our society than the latest dance step. Photography and athletics are different fields of endeavor, but when the two collide, everyone gets to see what only the Frederic Remingtons saw before. The same old problem of how to get a ball into a basket doesn't disappear, it simply becomes embedded in a new context. We watch old films and wonder at the primitiveness of games that at the time seemed sophisticated; after so many years uniforms look old. We never question what the camera shows our lives to have been. But the judgment "old" implies a discarded set of means to win at games. The changing relationship between eternal puzzles and ways to solve them is shown when cameras are turned on sport. Records are set, always set, they never stop being set. Will humans one day swim as fast as the seal, run as fast as a horse, lift weights like an ant, outjump even the flea? If they do, cameras will record it, and in the process, give us a new measure of human potential.

Back in class, Margaret Mead comes on the screen once more. The Dani move out across their fields. They have slain a member of the neighboring village and now must meet the other clan's vengeance. Uncontrolled excitement rushes through the room; there is no talking with this prelude to war. Warriors can see the faces of their enemies clearly. They are of the same culture, use the same weapons, and are known to each other by name even as they try to kill. The air fills with arrows. Battle is driven to frenzy by the yammering dialect, New Guinea version of "in your face!" answered by more yammering, more spears, more arrows arcing, then dodged. The sun fades behind a mountain. This field has no lights. Both sides retreat, but not so far that they can't hear one another, spend the twilight challenging, insulting by name, by family insinuations. Wounded are carried back to the village, arrows still hanging from their chests and buttocks. By firelight those arrows are cut out. All the Dani men have scars which glisten when smeared with pork grease. No one has lost his life. It's now the bottom of the first.

"The fact that it is ritualized war makes their grief no less real," says Margaret Mead as the film runs on in the dark. A young man has been ambushed and his body is being prepared for cremation. Women heave with forced sobs, one much more than the others; she must be the parent. It is a wracked village. No art, no music, no business or politics gets done when there is a funeral resulting from war. Logs are piled high into a pyramid up around the body seated in a chair of lashed sticks. The fire begins slowly then rushes up through the timbers. A pig for the funeral feast is held wrenching and squealing, then shot through the heart with an arrow, and falls convulsing into the dirt. Margaret Mead appears again. "It is this never-ending cycle of war, and more war, in which defeat must always be avenged, that has shaped the Dani culture for so many centuries." For them there is always a season, never a winner.

The decision to take camera in hand to photograph a child at play must have some unacknowledged intentions: My own game films would show, I hoped, things my eyes could not see. Maybe they would even reveal why, season after season, this child chases a ball, or how, after all the time and effort spent on sport, she might walk away from the game with a metaphor to use forever. Film showed the Dani caught up in a deadly cycle, unable, or perhaps unwilling, to break out. Surely in today's world a high school girl has overriding reasons for learning how to end such cycles, at the personal as well as social levels. Hope for deeper meaning guides the hand upon the shutter after all. Confidence, anticipation, the all-consuming individuality of an artist at work, accompany the sound of film being loaded.

Of course at first one tries to duplicate *Sports Illustrated*. Action! Hitting the layup! Arms tangled! Drama! But the best pictures are of her waiting to go in. She's kneeling, down on one kneepad in front of the scorer's table. No one knows the picture has been taken from across the court with a telephoto lens, or that a whole series of the same picture has been taken with various shutter speeds and light settings. The first one will be the best, the only one you can't look at enough to get its full impact, or resolve its incongruency—a brief time of studied silence in a rowdy fast-action game. The option to study fleeting moments must be the fascination with sports photography, with any photography. The statistician, timer, a reporter, are all looking toward the right. Somebody must have scored. Yet her attention is on the guard she must guard. It's the pause before a storm.

Only thoughts of tactics, strategy, and the movements that will follow, show on her face. In the car afterwards her little brother will say he loves to see her best move— the reverse anticipation steal followed by a full-court-fast-break-behind-the-back-dribble-left-handed layup. But I wonder about the effects of all this on the other team, the girls in red and gold. Will they go home tonight and plot revenge? If so, then they've taken one step into the world of the Dani. Now suppose they plot revenge knowing it's not a life or death matter, that they do indeed have the option to say enough of this cycle of conflict for higher and still higher stakes. Then they will have learned more from the Dani experience than the New Guinea warriors ever thought their culture could teach an American girl.

How absolutely trite it would be at this point to mention "it's not who won or lost . . . ," that worn out expression every loser knows so well. Better, perhaps, just to remember what we saw in the game films. No never-ending Dani cycle need await the girl down on a kneepad in front of the scorer's table. She may have a burning desire to win, but in the picture, one only sees recognition of a job to be done, her awareness of her role as a member of a team in this most "team" of team sports where speed and an infinite number of movements place a high premium on cooperation between players. Something in the opponents' style of play tells her the ball can be stolen, batted loose and rolling into midcourt, or stripped away from a guard who holds it too low. She flicks a glance at the officials; her eyes get very wide. The horn shatters the echo chamber that is every high school gym, and she is on the floor. Thief at work.

We later look at the pictures I was so sure would be in *Sports Illustrated.*

"Why didn't you take pictures of all the team?" I don't know why, now. It just didn't occur to me at the time. It was the only opportunity of a season. They'd played in the afternoon. One wall of the gym was glass brick that provided all the light you could ever want or need. But I took pictures only of her. She flips through the prints and settles on one.

"I don't hold my hands like that." Her fist is closed with the thumb inside. She's so much in the act of dribbling with her left hand that most of the picture is blurred, yet her right hand is a baby fist with the thumb inside. She's still a little girl playing ball.

Television, newspapers, and magazines bring into any house sports photography that conveys a range of information. We see every day the simple documentation of a pitch, a basket, a putt. As an exercise in trying to attach significance to athletics, few acts are as instructional as getting out last month's sports page, turning to the picture of a professional ballplayer, and asking yourself just how important it is for society to have a record of this particular instant. Daily journalism dwells in a universe of ephemeral and unique, but at the same time familiar, moments. Magazines sometimes approach art, even on purpose. Walter Iooss's photo essays bring out personal feelings about baseball, spring training, individuals isolated against a game's symbolic fence. Art is supposed to convey a message in which viewers' feelings play an integral and necessary part. But certain films call forth emotions, raise questions about a future, show a side of sport never seen by journalism. Only a select few get to see them regularly. These pictures have nothing whatsoever to do with art.

"I'm going to take you up to X-ray now." He is probably a former student of mine. He recognizes the name. She slides off the table and into a wheelchair and is gone. They don't accept people "up in X-ray" unless they are in a wheelchair, he says, so I wait. An ambulance arrives and a black athlete is wheeled in strapped to a stretcher, his workout clothes obvious under the blankets. He's put in the room across the hall and orderlies slowly begin undoing the straps. He's flat on his stomach, not moving. She comes back down the hall in her wheelchair. She's been up to X-ray in other cities. She knows these kinds of places, all the orthopedic supplies, most of the terminology, and she can tell you the different uses of impregnated tape, fiberglass, and angled scissors. She gets back on the table and the wheelchair leaves. Conversation drifts in from across the hall, too casual, it seems, for someone brought in an ambulance. Trainers move in and out of the room; you can tell who they are by their jackets. She straightens to hear, leans to see. The technician brings in her X-rays and clips them to a fluorescent panel on the wall. I turn on the lights and begin to study her bones. She tells me the angle at which these game films were taken. I see the text-book-perfect bones of youth. I am stunned at the health, the perfect fit, the growing surfaces, fascinated by the look at an athlete's skeleton, suspicious of what the doctor is going to say when he sees the same pictures. So often when we think of the anatomy of sport, only muscles come to mind.

"Dislocated elbow," says the doctor when he finally comes in, indicating the room across the hall with his head. "Says he just made varsity, now he has this elbow."

He shakes his head and studies her game films. There is instant communication between the patients in the two rooms; you can feel it in the hospital-smell air: Two superb competitors felled temporarily and now in the hands of people who see only one side of a game—the side that hurts.

"Nothing chipped or broken." Then he begins the talk she's heard over and over, this analysis of ankle injuries, how they will only get re-injured, how basketball wears the ankles, stretches ligaments, what can eventually happen. She suffers patiently through this lecture. So do I. "Stay off the ankle." He writes out his recommended treatment which includes no more basketball for a while.

At age fifteen, however, sitting on a table in orthopedics, she's already participating in a grand philosophical battle over who owns a person's, especially a woman's, body—doctors? coaches? the Church? husbands? corporations? In the past, the pain has been hers; she's listened carefully to experts then assessed their predictions and precautions against what her own nerves told her. As with the Dani films, pictures provide a context that show us what the issues really are. In this case, they reveal a very subtle but important difference of opinion over who can tell whom what to do and for what reason. As I said, we've been through all this before. I've listened to the explanations, watched her reaction, remembered what happened afterward. The person who bears the hurt, who's spent most of her life stressing muscles and joints, is the one who decides what can or can't be done. Some pay for directions; others pay for advice.

I sign the agreement that says I will file an insurance claim; they give me a copy. I'm ready to be home with a drink in my hand and a good book; it's that time of day. Her workday has just started after her schoolday has ended. The streets are winter glazed. I drive gingerly, dropping her off back at practice.

"I'll get a ride home with Jennifer."

"Be careful walking on the ice."

No matter how ephemeral the moment, or what the sport, her picture in the paper is a thrill. Once in preparation for a speech, I made a study of a week's worth of eighteen daily newspapers, including their sports pages, the objective being to determine exactly what communities were telling themselves about the world. My conclusion was that the quickest way to validate your accomplishments in the eyes of your neighbors is to get your picture in the paper. During the week the papers were published, one woman got her picture on every sports page. She'd run a mile and set a world record. Accompanying her were dozens of other pictures ranging from high school football players starting fall practice to businessmen on the town golf course.

I've learned to recognize our local photojournalists in a crowd, especially when they show up at a girls' game. I see them come in, start fiddling around with their cameras, then disappear among the fans. It's always amazing how they can stop the action in such poor light. Sometimes you see them standing around leaning on a wall, but when it's all over, and you've been watching the game so intently, you realize they're gone and you've never seen them take a picture.

It's only when you decide to take a couple of rolls yourself that you understand how photography detracts from your sense of wholeness of a game. Mixing destroys the art of one and the sense of the other. The times I've taken pictures turn out to be games I can't remember thirty seconds after they're over. While looking so intently at places where players are likely to be in focus, you miss their reasons for being there. The act of tripping a shutter blots out what happens afterward, at least for a few seconds, if not minutes. The viewfinder frames your perfect compositions being created and destroyed at whatever speed the particular game is played, but it also excludes all else. Behind a camera, you lose the development, the context, and the consequences of a highly complex set of events. At the end, you're left holding a couple of strips of negatives with which to reconstruct a unique history. Makes you wonder what besides sports you're viewing with a photographer's eye.

On the other hand, any picture can be hypnotic because of the meaning in the mind of a person who views it. Volleyball shots usually show action at the net, players spiking and blocking. Problems of focus are partly solved by the nature of a sport. In my study of newspapers, I discovered a disproportionate number of pitchers in the act of throwing, second basemen making double plays, and catchers colliding with runners. I suspect this kind of representation is characteristic of sports photography because action can be predicted at home plate, second base, backboards, nets, hurdles, and finish lines. That's why I find the in-between shots especially fascinating. They show a part of games not usually seen, yet essential to the action that follows.

Such a picture of Jena appeared one morning in the paper. Of all the events that occur in volleyball, this one was the least likely to happen at a designated spot. After all, teams try to confuse one another by hitting the ball into unexpected places; a photographer should be as easily fooled as opposing players. But in the picture she is fielding a serve, or a spike, whose trajectory could never have been predicted. The picture is a stop action of a very familiar set of movements: Both feet are slightly off the floor, the hair is bouncing—the fashion-required headband holds nothing—and the arms are extended, hands clasped, elbows locked, all in perfect concentration and form.

Karen cuts out the photo and sticks it up on the refrigerator with some magnets. Then copies begin to come in the mail, with notes. "Cute girl!" "Cute picture!" "Cute girl, cute picture!" "Congrats! Darling pic!" It is a cute pic, there is a darling girl in it. The evidence is there, undeniable. But all these clippings come from women who are close friends of the family. They are also women from a certain stage in the sociological evolution of their nation. They may be insulted by this analysis, but not one of their notes says "she looks like she's trying very hard to win." The freedom allowed by art—the luxury of seeing anything you want in it, or of assigning whatever meaning is in your mind—has demonstrated that these game films have a deeper significance than just the validation of one child's accomplishment (she did field the serve and get it into play properly). We may be free to interpret as we wish, but our wishes are structured by our values, and by the social forces that surround us. The notes reveal what was seen by our friends, or maybe, even more interestingly, what our friends thought we would like for them to say about our daughter's picture. Whatever the explanation, to the senders of these notes, it was important that she be cute. She is cute. She is darling. But she is also a precision machine determined like all living hell to win. You can see it in the game films.

The camera has been our microscope. Like that instrument, it also continues to broaden our view of the universe, but not without a cost. We pay for this expanded vision with our naïveté. Having seen beyond first impressions, we can no longer look upon a field or court, feign a quick analysis, then move on to other equally–disguised human endeavors. Instead, society around us comes to understand just how complicated, how metaphorical and allegorical, sport can be, especially when one adds context and history to the captured moment. In purporting to tell what is, the camera shows us what is not. In saying "this happened and here is the evidence," the camera actually says "this happened and now it is up to you to understand it, or give it meaning, for if you don't, others will."

We do not like to struggle too hard with things seen in the guise of entertainment: paintings, sculpture, dinosaur skeletons, trilobite fossils, movies, all such captured singularities. The camera's statement is a worthy challenge for those who would view game films, think they are seeing a child at play, then move on to other matters. We began with pictures of and a comment on the Dani by one who made her profession studying the human animal. We also end with a conclusion born of anthropology: An instrument of our own design, one that fixes moments and demands a context for the commonplace, shows us more about ourselves than we ever imagined. This is what there is to learn from game films.

5

Jordan Country

A number of years ago a man named Pat Jordan wrote a book entitled *False Spring*, a haunting description of the life of a young baseball player starting in the depths of the farm system. Pat Jordan went on to become a talented sports writer, his brief career as a pitcher providing the theme for *False Spring:* It is better to have tried and failed, than to spend the rest of your life wondering if you'd have been good enough. Jordan's verbal picture of ball parks, rickety wooden bleachers along the edges of small towns set on the high plains, the loneliness of hotel rooms in places like McCook, Nebraska, and life on the road at night, struck a familiar chord. I worked summers at a university's biological field station in that part of the country. I'd stood many times in a city park, the orioles' fruity calls drifting down from a canopy of clattering cottonwood leaves, looking out across a ball diamond, over the green wooden fence, to the Sandhills where cattle stood and the horizon turned to gray lavender below a burning sky. In my mind, Pat Jordan, just a kid, always stood on the mound and dust devils swirled up around second base.

In this same country one year, where no one thinks

much about driving thirty miles so a kid can play in a league with team names like "The Mets" or "The Cubs," Jena decided she would play hardball with the boys. She'd practiced with them once the previous year and they'd all wondered where that kid who could throw so hard came from. When she walked out of their lives that day they were still not sure whether she was a boy or a girl. Wouldn't be much of a question this year. Before the season was over they'd be calling her for dates to the one movie in town, chaperoned by a big sister who was old enough to drive. Jena also grew as tall as she would ever be that summer—five feet three, prairie-straw hair hanging out from under a baseball cap, light blue eyes searching over the diamond, almost as if she knew of a world beyond the infield, but wasn't ready to admit it. Somehow the fence enclosed a couple of acres of childhood. Grown-ups sat in the bleachers or watched from pickups.

There was no doubt in her own mind that she would make the team and play. She considered her ability to field a grounder off the dusty sand to be her ticket, and when you're twelve and a half you don't pay much attention to the administration of kids' baseball or the subtleties that go along with it. Her coach was a colleague of mine, another who'd come to the western plains to study animals, except in his case, he was unable to shake the effects of growing up too close to Cleveland. He wore a Cleveland Indians cap, several Cleveland Indians T-shirts, drank from a Cleveland Indians coffee cup, and scarcely hid his great longing for Bob Feller on his roster. In this part of the world, with this team, the closest he could come to the latter was a girl.

"I'm giving them until Thursday afternoon," said the coach, "to find me a ninth player before I take her." Their first game was Thursday night.

"Don't want anybody to accuse you of slipping them a ringer?"

"I just want to give them every chance to find me another player." He was a man with total respect for the order of both the world and the game, and sometimes equated the two. No group of boys, just learning where their feet were, ever walked away from a ball diamond with more respect for the game or a higher standard of sportsmanship on the field, than those he got by the luck of the little league spring draw. But this year the draw had given him only eight players. Anything played with fewer than nine cannot be called "baseball" no matter what the rules and equipment. The conflict in this man's mind was palpable. Baseball is played by men and boys; how long can one wrestle inwardly with the combination of girl and arm that were it not for tradition, might be considered talent? The answer is obvious: One can wait until Thursday afternoon, until the system has been given its chance, and more.

My only concern about this matter had to do with the chauvinist traditions that surrounded everything symbolized by baseball, ranches, cowboys, Cleveland Indians, and pickup trucks. Down deep, I sincerely hoped this whole generation of boys would not grow up with impressions of girls made of arms that can fire a baseball through the side of a freight train if necessary. Karen worried about her pitching, about the line drive through the mound, the one that knocked out permanent teeth. I was not ready for the inevitable batter hit by one of her screamers. I knew what they felt like in the glove; only a scientist's curiosity could make me wonder what they sounded like, against plastic, from inside a batting helmet. Coach took care of the worries; his judgment was accepted without question.

"None of these kids can throw hard enough to hurt anybody." In games, people often deceive themselves for purposes only they know. To think about the unpleasant destroys your concentration. Yet her tone of voice, and the softening of her face at the idea of one of her pitches against bare flesh, gave away her opinion of the adult conclusions. She would not have wanted to be hit by one of her own pitches. She knew how fast she could send a ball toward its dusty leather target, how hard she intended that ball to hit the glove held below a mask from which two eyes sought hers. Besides, to not throw a strike is a failure. But at twelve one still has a great deal to learn about baseball as a metaphor—while it would upset her to hit a batter, there were times she suspected they ducked a shoulder in front of a pitch just to get on base. That she saw as a failure of another kind.

She stayed at shortstop for the first game, which her team won, and through most of the second, which they lost by a good many runs. It was to be their last loss for several weeks, for after the second game the coach sent her to the mound in the fourth inning, a ritual that was to continue throughout the season. Pretty soon word got around the local bars that she was pitching. That's when her fan club appeared. It consisted of two graduate students: Steve and Rick.

Steve and Rick were pretty fast company, especially when they'd stopped by the Sip 'n' Sizzle on their way to the game. Coach might have taught her the rules and sportswomanship, but Steve and Rick taught her to take command of the mound like a grizzly bear from outer space. Not only that, but right there in the hometown intimacy of those four rows of aluminum bleachers, with parents and grandparents and other assorted relatives yelling kind and hopeful encouragement, Steve and Rick screamed at her to "blow it past them gra-a-a-vy suckin' pigs!" Underneath they might have been well-educated, intelligent and sensitive, but on the outside, especially at the ball park, and I suspect at any ball park, you'd have to look hard to find a tougher pair. Rick looked a lot like some country singer hawking chewing tobacco in a television commercial. Steve had been an athlete—played baseball and basketball—back in Indiana, before he'd come to Jordan country to write a doctoral dissertation on lizards. Together they worked out of the same field camp where all our children, because of my employment, often sat down at breakfast to deep discussions, with people twice their ages, on everything from nuclear war, theoretical ecology, the evolution of parasitic worms, to the previous evening's festivities at a local tavern.

Rumors spread among my professional acquaintances in other cities suggest that Rick has reformed since those days we shared in the Sandhills, but at the time he led the unhealthiest of all lives. Smoke curled up into his eyes from the ever-present cigarette crunched between his teeth. His mind knew no restrictions, had no respect for the barriers scholars erect around their various areas of special interest. He'd read all of Steinbeck, would look a snake right in the eye, and walked on frayed cuffs of ragged jeans every step of his convoluted way. Years later, Steve would be able to regale any audience with stories of his former companion. I have no doubt that somewhere in the world Rick is doing the same with his memories of Steve. They are both the stuff of legend; once when searching for the right body in which to put a fictitious character, I borrowed Rick's.

Steve was a little more refined than his sidekick, possibly because he'd found his life's focus: lizards. He chased them all day long, marking them, and noted their behavior, temperatures, weights, and sexes, in the blistering heat over sandy dunes a mile from shade or water. At the end of every such day, even the most dedicated need diversion. He chose as his the education of a ballplayer. "Tricks of the trade" came out over dinner, Jena's eyes getting larger and larger at the very idea that games had psychological components, which sometimes turned out to be more important than physical skills.

"This is how you rub the ball before each pitch," he demonstrated, glowering around the room from under lowered eyebrows. She picked it up immediately. Anyone who's danced ballet and played the piano for half her life can learn such movements in a flash. Steve passed along the secrets; Rick, puffing faster and faster, gasping "yeah! yeah!" at each new idea, validated them. Then on her own she added a bunch of other tricks, like shaking off a sign that was never given, carefully adjusting her fingers on the seams for a special pitch she'd never learned to throw, waving her defense to shift positions for a batter she'd never seen before, and advancing off the mound with that disgusted slight slouch, wrist on hip, mouth and nose wrinkled, as if by sudden stench, at an ump who'd failed to notice she'd clipped the inside corner. Coach didn't help much. He'd warm her up holding the glove out from his hand just to make it pop, then act like she'd dished up some real fire. The twelve-year-old catchers started doing the same, having trouble fielding her only pitch—the fastball, shaking their heads and giving worried last-rites looks at those hitting first in lineups. The game within the game: If it hadn't been so serious it wouldn't have been so funny.

None of this would have worked if it hadn't been for the fireball. I'd discovered it was real the last time we'd played burnout. The ball came down a hundred feet of yard slightly wild, around my glove, across the street, up a driveway and into a garage door, rattling windows and sending occupants out onto the lawn like ants stirred with a stick. That was the last time we played burnout. In Pat Jordan country, I decided she'd made her point for the season, win or lose, when a kid from another team said "I'm the fastest pitcher in the league next to Jena."

She played for the Astros, who weren't supposed to win much. The Mets were also pushovers, but the Expos were tough. At least that was the word circulating around town before she came to the mound. The Cubs showed promise but never seemed to put it all together. That was their league before the second game, the one on Tuesday with the Mets, which the Astros were supposed to win easily— practice for the rampaging Expos the following week. But coaches' grown-up game plans don't always materialize when little league takes the field. She stayed at shortstop until it was too late, until the doormat Mets were a dozen runs ahead. Shortstop seemed her natural habitat; the beauty of her fielding a grounder and leaning into the long throw to first made a parent misty. Then she left shortstop, came to the mound that first time in a game long lost, and started throwing a few warm-ups. All the frustration of a team twelve runs behind the league pushover was in every pitch. Even the umpire flinched a little bit, and ducked, when a ball clipped the catcher's mitt and ricocheted off the cage, skittering in the dust as the batter's eyes pleaded for a "ball." The bleachers were pretty silent at the end. Folks were not sure what had been uncovered.

The big Expos brought their winning streak to the park on Thursday and struck out dutifully, ending up eight or ten runs behind the Astros as bewildered clean-cut boys in purple shirts picked up their things and headed for the Dairy Queen, and an equally bewildered but determined coach started looking for help among the available unoccupied town kids. The second meeting between these two teams was a high-pressure cliff-hanger. The Expos fielded some bigger boys; the game ran late, ending with the Astros ahead 14-13, Jena on the mound, bases loaded, two outs, as she blew it past the last Expo for her strikeout.

"She plays better under pressure," said Karen. But when asked about games afterward, Jena has always told the details, an insider's analysis of the movements and strategies, rarely the feelings. Evidently, when it's time to play, it's also time to pay very close attention to what is going on around you. Such a need for concentration may not allow many feelings until the end. Get too mad and you lose perspective; get too happy and you forget to watch the others. Even in Jordan country, at that age, playing well under pressure meant her mind was on her business. On the mound with two outs, a run ahead, and the bases loaded behind you, is no place for a girl to get scared. Instead, it's a place to think with all your might about every move.

"The Expos have been recruiting," said the coach's wife with an ominous sound, as if recruiting were not something a person should do in a town like this, kind of in the same league as starting a tornado.

But the Expos had talent, skills, and size, which began to show late in the season. They fielded with confidence, swung on about everything, and got their hits. By the time it came down to the final tournament game on a blistering Sunday afternoon—these two teams facing one another in hundred-plus-degree sun—the pitching troubles that had plagued them all season had been solved. From somewhere had come an unusual number of boys in purple shirts, and the Expos' starting pitcher, the one the Astros had belted out of the park in the early going of two previous games, stayed harmlessly out of the way on second base.

The last tournament game, for the league championship, came laced with kaleidoscopic impressions: heat waves out between the mound and second; the unearthly clang of an aluminum bat; a belted drive ending up in a second baseman's glove with his foot on the bag for an unassisted double play; Jena waving off the infield on a pop fly while some guy in the stands muttered "she *is* surehanded." Between late innings, coach stood in the dirt telling a bench of orange-shirted Astros that they'd "scored ten runs in a single inning before and could do it again," but it was not to be. The Expos stuck it to the Astros but good, and were ecstatic—yelling, jumping, standing tall and proud over their league championship, telling themselves they'd won when it counted. Jena was disgusted. But she'd gotten her share of strikeouts and the sportswomanship she'd learned in the short season allowed her to keep her perspective.

"So the Expos beat the Astros one out of three," I said, "not a bad performance, win a third of the time."

"You pitched well, Jena," said Karen, "you blew it past them gravy suckin' pigs." We all smiled at the memory of a couple of students out to cheer a little girl, win or lose, of a coach who put the game itself above victory, of baseballs against a prairie sky at sunset, and a town that came to watch on Tuesdays and Thursdays. Years later when asked about the Astros, she'd say they "seemed awfully professional," then follow with mention of the trip to the Dairy Queen after practice. Somehow the ideas suggested by "professional" and "Dairy Queen" aren't very congruent nowadays. I suspect the "professional" derived from her coach's expectations: he knew of nothing else to ask from a student, or player, other than attention, dedication, courage, and all-out effort. The "Dairy Queen," of course, came from the fact that everyone was, after all, just a kid.

My job for the summer was over; we'd stayed in the

Sandhills, three hundred miles west of home, a day longer than in past years, just to watch a final game. Then, just like that, it was time to leave, one minute the sounds of baseball, the next a car engine coughing into life and the click of seat belts. She threw her glove into the back of the station wagon and settled down for a six-hour drive. Before long we were out of that country where dunes march to the horizon, and late that night she was on the telephone to her best friend for the first time in a month and a half, talking not about games, but about experiences with wild animals, live birds held for a time, lizards, and college students who talked to her about things not many twelve-year-olds learned. The next day she would return to her softball team, a mild activity indeed compared to the intensity of real baseball in a league with boys, the Mets, Cubs, Astros, and now-champion Expos. She sat on the bench most of her first softball game in six weeks, courtesy of another coach who also loved the game but understood the need for those who'd stayed at home to get their chance before the one who'd been away. She finally took the mound.

"Underhanded!" I yelled. She laughed.

"Blow it past them . . ." said Karen, then stopped. We were back in the city.

Life went on for a few days, then came a letter.

"Jena got a letter from Eric," I noticed.

"It's the second one she's received from him," said Karen, adding, "the first time he said he wished she were still out there."

"Baseball season's over."

"He wanted to take her to the movies again."

Years after that season in the Sandhills, I walked into a university classroom to teach my course in beginning biology. Two or three hundred students filed in, took their places among rows of padded seats, and settled down for fifteen weeks of boredom, excitement, frustration, success, failure, whatever their backgrounds and interests would allow from a sampling of scholarly pursuits. Among their names was that of a young man from my past. Four weeks went by before I handed back some papers, finally coming to his. He reached for the answer sheet, but I held it.

"Where are you from?"

He smiled and answered—Pat Jordan country.

"I caught for your daughter."

Later he came to my office. We talked about plans, aspirations, attempts to succeed in situations structured by forces other than your own, and over which you don't have total control. In a few months I heard he'd left the university. I was saddened by the news, and a little frustrated, but it reminded me of some thoughts I'd had on the way home that blistering afternoon so many years ago when the Expos won their championship: Most of these kids had come as close to the game of baseball as they'd ever hope to come, but none had failed to carry away everything it had to offer on a hot and dusty afternoon, thunderheads gathering in the west, in that place where a young man named Pat Jordan once began to lose at sport and win at life.

6

Angels

*C*onflicting images wrought by overlapping seasons, multiple sets of shoes, and a bewildering array of equipment designed to control numerous kinds of balls, come to every parent who has a young child skilled at games. Softball, volleyball, basketball, tennis, track, softball . . . then it is summer again, is the cycle of those caught up in sport by virtue of their offspring's talents. Exceptions occur, of course. Competitive swimming, the most allegorical of age group pursuits, precludes most else—by ten one is a potential champion, at fourteen a junior national record is dinner-table conversation, and at twenty-five, swimmers are old men and women. But the need for a team forces patience upon sport, so ball is somewhat less binding than a young life in fast lanes marked by lines and floats. Besides, hand/eye coordination is a commodity of value to many games, while the unique movements of butterfly and backstroke can be expressed only in one environment. At twelve, a girl can still come home, shoot baskets on the driveway for a while then adjourn to the backyard for a little burnout with dad and never think twice about the transition.

None of this activity continues for very long, however, without a coach. Somebody always stands along the side of a court, or a pool, or track, and yells, points, then calls another aside for a few words or gestures. Information is conveyed by means of actors' skills. Player watches, coach performs; coach watches, player performs, then both repeat their roles until it's time to play for keeps, when coaches learn how well they've taught and players are taught how well they've learned, and each begins to understand how satisfying it is to see potential converted into the reality of a performance. This is why coaches are sometimes remembered longer than other teachers: Nobody stands by and shows you the way a pencil is to be moved to solve an algebra problem; no crowd cheers at the final derivation. Instead, a single mind wrestles all alone in silence with symbols, relationships, and the logic of substitution.

The few whose adrenalin flows at the thought of a calculus exam become mathematicians. The many who feel the same chemistry anticipating ball games become players. But when play time is over, those who still demand the sense of being called into a game become coaches. Some coaches then develop into teachers. They are referred to by the media, and remembered by their players, as "successful." Newspapers call them successful because they win; players because they're remembered, such as the two whose stories follow.

Larry works for IBM and lives by the lake. He also looks a little bit like the Dallas Cowboys' Tom Landry and dresses as if he were on his way to pose for an ad in *Esquire*. He is a former athlete. Down by the track one day I stood near to where he finished his workout. He could still run with power, the pounding of his feet spelling the difference between spectator and competitor. Competitors enter a world that only they can know, when they take to track, court, or pool with their bodies and their minds. I remember thinking, if I decided to run around that quarter-mile asphalt oval, it wouldn't sound like Larry. He and his wife, Carol, have two daughters, Amy and Cori. Carol has always been the administrator, the "Commissioner of Athletics," the financial wizard at motels and restaurants. Larry has always coached—his kids and their friends.

Larry taught basics. He drove a car with personalized license plates that said FIRST. He didn't intend to be anything else. Neither did the girls who came to play for him. That was one of the basics. Their sponsors were a vending company—Tom's Foods; their colors red, white, and blue, and the game, basketball. All this started when we took a child to play in elementary school gyms on Saturday mornings. A lot of snow was tracked in, coats were piled in the corners, and moms and dads supplied the good-natured yelling at tiny people running up and down the floor. At some point Larry must have decided: I'm going to coach a basketball team. Then came the sponsor. After all these years it's difficult to pin down the exact set of events. Instead, it seems like Tom's foods has always sponsored a team called the Angels; Larry has always been the coach, Carol the manager, and Jena the point guard.

There are memories of increasingly better gyms, some with PA systems, others with lighted scoreboards, one or two filled with hostile crowds, refs making quick exits. The Angels grew close-knit, thriving on coordination, skills, coaching dignity, kindness, the giving of enormous resources of time and talent. And victory. Tom's Angels won and won, occasionally lost, but by and large won. Toward the end it was obvious something more than basketball had happened.

What was that "something more"? It was the product of

a person who'd learned respect for a game because of what it could give him and who, probably without much of a struggle over the act, decided to try to pass along the opportunity for others to do the same. Viewed objectively, Larry just volunteered to mix a few basketballs with the knowledge of where to run and how to hold your arms, an indescribable quality which, for lack of a better phrase, I'll call "general approach to a problem," and thirteen or fourteen young ladies of various preteen ages. He then added phone calls requesting the use of church or school gyms, or asking parents to drive. Somehow by doing all this he generated an abstract product known as a "team." People are as solid as their uniforms, but "teams" are not. How many times have you read a coach's complaint "we weren't a 'team' tonight?" Plenty. But Larry constructed a team using ethereal tools—his tone of voice, manner of dress, and the way he dealt with officials when the girls were watching. A man who earned a living selling office machinery became, on his time off, a teacher.

I would like to go back a few years now and mention a situation which might seem, at first, to have little bearing on the fate of Tom's Angels. One event, however, is common to both Larry's actions and those of the person I am about to describe—the decision to coach. This coach, and he was generally acknowledged as a highly successful one, was seventy years old when I met him. He'd had national championship teams, the glory of a long, exciting career at one of the nation's premier universities, friends all over the world, and a summer sports camp in Canada. He'd had the experience of having been an Olympic coach, and he recruited just by answering his fan mail.

We met in a building that was one of the world's truly cold places. It was basically an uninsulated old wooden barn erected over steel beams. High in the rafters hung furnaces, or blowers, that only seemed to make the place colder in the sleet-glazed Oklahoma winters. The floor was small white tile, icy to bare feet. The starting blocks were high wooden crates that left you stunned and stinging for the first few strokes. A smell—chlorine—and a sound—the slamming of a three-meter board—joined the cold to cement these images forever in your mind. Above it all there was a voice, that of Matt Mann, calling out your life numbers from a stopwatch. We never took those numbers at face value, though they determined our roles. We always felt that when we needed to think we were going faster, Matt would tell us a lower time, and vice versa. In practice it's more important to realize your potential than to beat your roommate. Matt had a million ways to use his watch for bringing out your best. He sensed, and his swimmers quickly learned, that practice times are as relative as Einstein's space. Standing shivering in that icy barn, you knew you were being "developed."

Matt Mann had been faced with a life decision, at seventy, that few have the opportunity to make. I've wondered ever since meeting him what a person can do as a college student to prepare for such a choice. His home, the cultural as well as physical environment in which he'd built his life, was Ann Arbor, Michigan, and the University of Michigan, where he coached the men's swimming team. When he reached the age of seventy, a proven talent in a very competitive game, he was forced to retire. I'm sure there were ceremonies, cards, letters, gifts, and congratulations from friends. I'm just as sure none of them answered Matt's question: What do I do now? I cannot believe any of those well-wishers said "go to Oklahoma."

But that's what he did, evidently in response to the University of Oklahoma's offer of a coaching job. Oklahoma is a place where athletics are often a priority. It's also a place where undaunted confidence led an administrator to say that if Michigan is stupid enough to throw out talent just because it's reached the age of seventy, then Oklahoma is smart enough to pick it up for a song. So Matt was given a choice of sentence: Idleness in the comforts of home or work in a foreign land. He chose the work and the foreign land. He had no idea what he would find when he got there. What he found was the likes of me, plus the aging remnants of the South African Olympic team, and a truly spectacular wisp of a kid from Wichita. He walked into that decrepit cold barn one day and asked each of his un-known commodities to swim a couple of laps. Then he said:

"Well, you've each got two arms and two legs."

I know now that arms and legs, and lungs, are not equal. But his statement, which was to become a catch phrase in the years that followed, spoke only of potential. I wonder now if Matt came to Oklahoma on the faith that when business is the conversion of human potential into reality, then there is work to be done anywhere.

In the thirty years since Matt Mann retired as UM swim coach, my own life has progressed along some exceedingly fortunate roads. College degrees came fairly easily; Karen and I managed to stay married; I was always able to find a reasonably well-paying job doing something I loved. But those thirty years also brought an education in the admin-istrative workings of large universities, in the thoughts that populate the minds of people who spend their lives with students, and in the fates of successful teachers at the ends of their careers. From that experience I feel able to reconstruct the mental struggle that must have accom-panied Matt's decision. Life offers few greater thrills than that of seeing your pupils succeed. The sense of satisfaction that accompanies this occasion is deep, lasting; you feel a personal involvement in a grand and timeless human endeavor: instruction. Of all the things a person loses in retirement, it must have been this opportunity to see a kid you've coached come in first, that in the end drove Matt to Oklahoma. He had no idea there would be a national champion on his team. As it turned out, there were a few. But what he did know is that he'd have the chance once more to do his best, to pass along the knowledge, and to direct the efforts toward a goal, that would in the final fraction of a second, end with a splash, a gasp, and the click of a watch.

Of course parents love to see their kids win, at anything and everything. Hell knows no demon like the man whose kid does his or her best for a consistently losing team. Matt wasted no time with parents; there were swimmers and nonswimmers and parents fell into the latter category. Besides, when we get to college, we're supposed to be above all that little-league pettiness. Larry, however, had no choice but to deal with parents. For one thing, two of the bits of raw material with which he worked were his own, which meant that he had to be both teacher and father. Watching Larry balance the two, sometimes conflicting, roles, made you realize just how strong the desire to win is, compared to the need to teach.

It is no wonder, I thought many times, that a person who views the world in terms of converting human potential into reality can sort through the emotional debris of defeat in order to find an accomplishment. Neither is it any surprise that those who've never taught have little patience with a loss. After studying Larry and Tom's Foods' Angels through easy, relaxed, grade-school years, when games were only fun, through the increasingly serious middle grades when it became important to win, then finally into high school, when it became imperative to work your hardest to win, you could only come to feel that in the struggle between parent and teacher taking place inside one human being, the teacher was sensing victory.

There comes a time, Jena says, near the end of a basketball game, when the winner is no longer in doubt. She also says this is one of the best times, especially in close games, when you know the other team cannot beat you with a last second desperation shot from half court. Ten seconds to go with a five-point lead and possession of the ball turns out to be more satisfying, in many ways, than the final buzzer. When sport finally got so serious around our house that I found myself getting philosophical, asking the rhetorical question: Of what value is this activity in which we've invested so much time and money, I focused my attention on Larry and Carol. When did it become evident to them that in this matter of girls running up and down a basketball court, Tom's Foods and the Angels had a symbolic five-point lead with ten seconds to go in some larger game and possession not of a ball, but instead of an approach to the world of competition, wins, losses, and efforts that seem to have no immediate payoff? Just when was it, I wondered, that Larry realized the teacher had won.

I think it was when his own children reached high school. Cori didn't make varsity either as a sophomore or junior. As a junior she ended up with her face on the floor a hundred and fifty miles from home, in a reserve game, and from there to the hospital and dental surgeon. We were late on that trip, walking in while the reserves were still out on the floor, wondering where Cori was, then seeing Larry leading her out along the other side of the court, his hand on her arm, her hand to her mouth. As a senior, Cori decided not to go out for basketball. I see her now periodically on the university campus; she seems to be handling the complex matter of playing at college student without much effort. Then came Amy. Tiny Amy didn't make varsity as a sophomore either, at the final cut, but moved up right before the first varsity game. She was an accomplished thief, an ornery outside shooter, and was growing rapidly. I see Amy on campus too; like Cori, she seems to be taking college in stride. It is impossible to pin down the exact effects Tom's Angels had on these two. But I also see hundreds, maybe thousands, who don't handle pressure, disappointment, success, the demands of teamwork quite so easily as Cori and Amy. Then I wonder if these hundreds ever played for a coach they'd always remember, even if it was their own dad.

For several years, Larry called his team together late in the spring, after the school season was over, for the AAU tournaments. When everybody was ten years old it was easy. Because of the City Rec season, winter passed more quickly than if basketball had not been a part of our lives, and by the time Larry took the Angels to the Milford tournament you could see ducks far off over the horizon, over the corn stubble and short green wheat. Milford always meant a real gym, with scoreboards and lights, when everyone was just a kid. Then one year it was different. Along with bodies grew attitudes, ambitions, loyalties to a neighborhood, to what the neighborhood symbolized, to a boyfriend, an awareness of adult responsibilities looming on the horizon with geese in the spring, a startlingly close view of the end of an idyllic but stressful time—high school—and above all the sight of a world in which, suddenly, ideas count for more than baskets.

The skill with which Larry had done his coaching job began to come back to him in ways he'd not envisioned. The City Rec league had no boundaries; recruits could come from anywhere to find the coaching skills their parents thought they needed. Public schools were different; they lay in the middle of districts with physical limits that in turn brought loyalties. And rabid fans. And state championships and sports page coverage by reporters who never forgot which city school they went to. And colors. And rivalries that went back to when parents played and wore those same colors on their jerseys. And coaches who fed on all of the above and who didn't stir the public ire the way teachers who belong to unions do. And Larry sitting strangely calm and thoughtful in the stands as two Angels take their places in the center circle, on opposite sides of the line, Jena takes her defensive position, and the ball goes into the air.

These are the timeless memories of childhood. Amy and Cori played, but not necessarily the whole game. When dad is the coach it's evidently important to learn that one doesn't always get to play. Peggy had a way of popping it in from the corner. Lindy always fought underneath the basket and sometimes came away bruised. Karen was often high scorer. Tonia's eyes used to get very big when she went on the court. Julie and Jody gave the game an uncharacteristic touch of grace and gentleness. Kim talked and everybody laughed. The other Julie always seemed to sink a long one in the clutch. Ann and Christy and Pam were some of the newcomers. And when things seem to fall apart in places when they should hang together, Jena wishes with all her heart she could turn back the clock and put on that red and blue home jersey with the number 34 on it.

7

~

Jungleball

*W*e spent a year one time, back in New Jersey, where I
had my first real job which paid what seemed like a for-
tune but was still not enough to retire both the loan we'd
taken out to get there and the hospital bills that arrived
shortly after a five-and-a-half-pound baby we named
Jenifer. A volleyball net stood behind the apartment complex where we lived. The previous occupants, necessarily
transient as all who study at universities are, had evidently chosen volleyball to bind themselves into a small
society. Most summer evenings whole families would play,
but once in a while four guys would get up on a Saturday
morning for a two-on-two ram-it-down-their-throats re-
lease of all the frustrations of people away from home. Afterward we'd sit around and drink some beer. I always
assumed that was the nature of the game: Wives and kids
got to play in the evening after dinner and every so often
the men would find time to blow away their aggressions
against one another. Then it would be safe again for
women and children. We never had the right number of
players, never knew, much less enforced, all the rules, but
called it volleyball anyway. I wondered even then how

much a game could be stripped of its formalities and still be recognized.

A dozen years later, after a move to one of the prairie states, I found myself wondering the same thing again at a university's biological field camp where we spent the summer. The isolation of a field station a mile down a dirt road from a minor highway, ten miles from the hospital, with a single phone and no television, imposes a unity built on respect for those you might not notice otherwise in the city. Someone would always be polite to a faculty wife; out in the jungle she might have to give you a haircut. And when volleyball is the glue that holds this kind of temporary society together, forcing cooperation on different combinations of people night after night, when games become binding social forces, it's infinitely more important to play than even to win. But why volleyball? Because deep in the lakeside canyons ringing with a magpie's call there is no Student Health, no Student Union, no Program Council to support with student fees. So the Rec Department bought a volleyball net and some big steel poles and sent them out on the next pickup truck headed west. Later on they sent some grass, not the kind you smoke, but the kind you plant because it's supposed to grow back over the "court" during the winter so a big blowout won't start and send the lodge down the hill.

Biology camp begins to loosen up about the second or third day; everybody is just learning everyone else's name and starting to wonder what there is to do in the boonies besides study toads. Then someone drags the net out of a box behind the pop machine. Another asks about a pump, finds it just where it was left the year before, and digs through a box of balls to see if one might hold air. A few of the girls get coaxed out into the grass which within a week will be worn down to hard hummocks. If the fall and spring weather have been right there'll be a hummock, right under the net, that you can stand on to get another three inches on your spike. The faculty kids don't need to be coaxed; they go squirting out between the legs of those big college guys and take their places over near where the lizards run. The joking and volleys "just to try it out" start. Invariably some coed plays with her hands clasped, arms extended and elbows locked, swinging upward with calculated concentration. In the jungle she's always considered a little strange. It's taken a while but I finally understand what is really happening: She's been involved with formal volleyball some time in the past, and carried away skills that she can't, or won't, forget.

Under casual circumstances—and there are few places more casual than a biological research station in a rural area—accommodations are made for wives, girls, little kids, old professors. Accommodations reveal the irreducible elements of any game. It's all right to call it volleyball so long as no person hits twice in a row, neither side hits more than three times, and the ball stays within boundaries marked by survey flags and a canyon full of cactus spines and yucca. Sides still rotate, of course, because rotation is an irreducible element. Matches end when evening classes start, the sun goes down, or lightning strikes nearby. Time-outs are called for spectacular sunsets and unusual birds. By unspoken agreement, talent and faculty kids are divided up evenly.

Occasionally a person who cannot stand to lose comes to summer camp. Why does this person not seem to fit into the jungle game while back in the city he or she would set the standard by which other players would be judged? Back there, the failure to accept the idea of defeat would make such a player the one who sets standards of performance. In the city we adore winners—they are the ones with the daily headlines. Could it be that in the midst of rock wrens and bull snakes, winning is shown not to be an irreducible element of the game? Jungleball casts an interesting light on athletics. When a game must be reduced to its base elements out of necessity, an ultimate truth is revealed: It is more important to play than to win. The game itself is more fundamental than victory. That there be a victor is crucial, for without it a game loses some of its structure, its pace, its underlying assumptions. But in the field the question is not "how do I win?" Instead, one asks: How do we put together this ragtag bunch, sides chosen out of social grace, in order to play respectably?

Jena takes the field. Once she was a "kid"; this year she'll be "talent." She'll also play with her hands clasped, arms extended and elbows locked, swinging upward with that calculated concentration. The other "talent" had then better pick up its responsibilities. When she puts the ball in the air, in a certain place, then that ball next belongs on the ground on the other side of the net. For her, this principle is an irreducible element of the game.

A smile is on her face. Her kitchen duties have been traded to another and the evening light still lingers. It's ball in the jungle. She's made a successful transition; for three months it will be more important to play than to win. But something is in the air that was not present in the gone-away childhood summers. A hangover persists, from her exposure to formal volleyball. Fingertip sets follow markings of territory; her voice is command; "mine" also establishes "yours," for she plays the sequence among the hackers. There may be flailings, rollings in the dirt, cowboy boots and bare feet pounding at cactus, many arms in the net, and long billed curlews high in the yellow western sun, but still she plays the sequence. She brings to jungleball the movements embedded in her mind and muscles last fall, when tension strung the air as tightly as the net. In a dream, a video, any surreal mix of scenes, the hills could fade into a gym, the grass into boards, deer tracks into a line, and still she'd field the serve, expect your hit across the net, and slip beneath your feet to bump the blocked spike safely into play. It makes no difference now, where she is. Like everyone who's learned anything from games, she carries her movements into places no one ever thought of when they threw a kid a ball.

What's it like to be on the court with your own daughter? You will never know for sure, but you can get a taste of it out in the jungle. She tolerates no misunderstanding, at least for long, about where a ball is supposed to go, or who has responsibility for fielding serves, or the uncertainty of adults in games they play once a year. To be on the field with someone who knows, truly knows, a sport is to suddenly realize what it means to be on a team, rather than among a collection of stumblebums, for she adds the sequence of hits and moves to her list of irreducible elements and your jogging shoes make strange tracks in the dusty sand next to hers.

Back in civilization, public school practices start the last week of August and, after the informality of summer, we fail to take the game seriously. Girls who play volleyball can't play tougher sports, we think, not knowing at the time the word is "won't" not "can't." But while true volleyball shows itself to be sophisticated beyond description, somehow the sand and sun make us unwilling to accept this demonstration. Maybe we don't want the summer to end, or are frightened somehow of formal volleyball, symbolizing for us the end of childhood times when games were reduced to their barest essentials. Formal volleyball is so filled with reducible elements that I'm surprised it's not classified as government service. It's no longer sport, perhaps, but higher education, a young girl's most trying exercise in learning to beat the system.

Seniors play, juniors warm the lowest row of bleacher seats, and sophomores play junior varsity. That is the first system to beat, for although she is a sophomore, she does intend to make varsity and play. It was not to happen. There is a reserve team for sophomores. If a sophomore wants to play, let her play reserves. So be it; she'll play reserves to the limit. She accepts her fate then goes to business.

We are here to play ball, to play ball; whistle, ref, direct the spherical traffic; I serve; the point is ours—that is an irreducible element I will add to your Confucian rulebook that governs what young women in uniform may do in public. You have so many rules they must have been acquired at birth, or like your language woven into your identity and spoken without forethought. With such a supply you will not even notice if I add one more: I serve; the point is ours; it's all so simple, ref, whistle now, and I will then serve the ball over the net, at which time it will curve slightly at high velocity, graze the head of that number two as she ducks, then hit the line for our first of fifteen quickies. Bam!

The game has a touch of dance: A pair of officials choreographs the rhythm that envelops a grandstand of parents, grandparents, boyfriends, for in this part of the country at this time of day no one else shows up to watch the reserves. The sounds echo from steel beam rafters up among the lights. Even the warm-up is ritualized: Four minutes this, four minutes that, four minutes the other thing, now we play. See that girl, so good in warm-up? She will not live up to her potential in the game, for she's not learned to get around the system. See her serve? It will hit the net in the game. See those sets? They'll be too far from the net. That setter has yet to defeat her fear of the rules. See that spiker leap so high, slam the ball upon the floor? She'll fault in the game, for her mind is free now only because it is warm-up and in a few moments her thoughts will be on the error. So here is the real struggle, the game within the game. Young women who plant seeds upon this field of friendly strife may harvest mental freedom on other fields and in other times.

'The court is sixty feet long by thirty feet wide, including all boundary lines, which are two inches wide and clearly visible. The net is three feet wide and thirty-two feet long when stretched taut. It is made of four-inch-square mesh and bound on all sides by a two-inch canvas tape. Cable or rope is threaded through the tape to enable the net to be fastened and pulled tight. The top of the net should be level and measure at the center of the court seven feet four and a half inches for women and girls.'

So these are the dimensions of my life today: sixty by thirty by two by seven plus four and a half. Are there any games we play that do not take place within boundaries? Are limits an irreducible element of sport? Without limits, is there sport? The width of a line—the ball on the line, point or side out, the ball outside the line, point or side out. Must we define even the width of the boundary to provide a fixed basis for what must inevitably be a judgment call? What about in the summer jungle—are the lines the width of a bull snake? And as straight? The plane that separates me from my opponents—if I can't go under it, why doesn't it go to the floor? Is this only one more subtle way of making it more difficult to obey a rule? Is a four-inch-square hole large enough for me to see my opponent, see the look on her face, the determination, the uncertainty? Seven feet four and one half inches is 1.4047619 times five feet three; is that accurate enough for a description of what it takes for me to put a ball over that net? Is the half inch necessary? Is it enough? Blow your whistle, ref, direct the traffic. I serve; the point is ours. Can that rule be expressed in feet and inches and fractions? . . . Can it?

'The volleyball is spherical with a twelve-or-more piece leather or rubber case. It must not be less than twenty-five inches or more than twenty-seven inches in circumference, and weigh not less than two hundred fifty grams or more than two hundred eighty grams. The case is inflated with not less than seven pounds or more than eight pounds of air pressure for the leather case; not less than five pounds or more than thàn seven pounds pressure for the rubber case. The ball should be balanced.'

Now which of the twelve or more leather pieces of the case do I slam the heel of my hand against tonight? Is it the one with the label, or do I turn the label toward that girl on the back row so that the letters come looming at her? How much superstition should I allow myself on this matter of where to hit the ball? Would not any one suffice to pound with all the force to make this white mass of somewhere between two hundred fifty and two hundred eighty grams dance upon the silent air until it skips her wrist and lays its eight pounds pressure, or is it seven, or seven and a half, upon the two-inch line? At last I have a choice—which piece to hit. It seems so strange, so unlike this game, to have a choice. Do I deny even this by deciding it does not matter which I hit? And is there a hidden rule that makes a farce of my independence? If I choose the wrong one can the dynamic principles of flow and drag and lift make a mockery of my willed trajectory? The ball should be balanced. That I can handle, ref. The ball will be balanced on the fingertips of my left hand. Should they also be measured, and placed in position before I smack this ball with all my might right at that kid across the net? Direct the traffic, ref; I serve and the point is ours. Measure the circumference of that.

'When the ball is served, every player must be within her playing area as determined by the serving lineup. All forward line players must be in front of all back line players, and no player's feet may overlap an adjacent player's feet at the instant the ball is contacted for the serve. Players are not allowed to serve out of turn. This error may be called by the scorer or by the opponent's captain or coach, and any points made on the service are cancelled and a side out declared.

A point shall be scored for the serving team when its opponent makes an error or commits a foul.'

What is this overabundance of musts, list of errors, catalog of fouls, scroll of punishments, lexicon of penalties, almanac of cancellations and this . . . this . . . watchful eye of scorers, linesmen and coaches, referees, umpires, and timekeepers whose decisions are final? Is all this taboo necessary for girls to play ball? What kind of game is this, ref, where points are scored because someone fails in an attempt at something? Of what value is this sport as a model for my life? Why is this such women's work? Is there no way to write your rules so they speak of accomplishment instead of foul? "The server shall balance the ball on her left fingertips, put a fiery concentrated look on her face, place her right hand against the back of her head as if to guide it with thoughts that are in her mind, look straight down her arm, and slam the ball with the heel of her hand with all the force at her disposal. If those across the net are lucky or good enough to return the service, then the server shall move, take the pass, and set it perfectly so the hitter can then place it on the floor across the net." See? There is not a "not" in that entire set of rules, only a list of accomplishments. Whistle, ref; I serve and the point is ours.

'If a player re-enters the game in a different position, she may not remain unless she assumes her original position. If the discovery is made before the opponents serve, points scored by her team while she was playing the wrong position are cancelled and a side out declared. When a sub-stitute player replaces a fourth-entry player or a wrong-position player, it is counted as an entry even though she may be the player replaced by the fourth-entry or wrong-position player.'

Only four entries? How many times can, or may, we enter the bigger games, ref? Is four enough, or do we do it every day of every week of all seasons until that final time we lie down for scavengers and our substitute steps up to take our place? Or do we do it only once, a single chance, a single serve that's either good or bad, or fielded by the others, or missed? What is so magic about four? Or position? These are my positions for entry into this game of can'ts and nots and watchful eyes: crouched, waiting, swaying, for the serve no one can hit hard enough to cause me to flinch; or a ref's hairsbreadth away from the net, my feet so firm, my fingers spring, for a ball that could be red-, no, white-hot, and never singe the hands that place the perfect set; or laid out flat upon the floor in a diving chase to save possession of the ball. Or I'll slip below the feet of hitters—let the blocked shot fall, I'll save it, play it off the net.

But most of all, my right position is standing three steps behind the line. From there I see her face, through the net, through that space between the balanced ball and the palm of my left hand. That's where I'll hit this serve, at what I see in the palm of my hand. It will be our point. I have played beneath the golden sunset and in between the spiny cactus, ref, where no one cares about fourth entry, but this serve will be our point. That final rule is an irreducible element of what I now do among the watchful stares of those who'd see me err—direct the traffic, ref; I serve; the point is ours.

'The server may not unnecessarily delay serving, nor serve too suddenly.'

I will serve just right.

'Decisions of officials are final.'

Volleyball may indeed be the most sophisticated of games with spheres. Of all the times parents get undone over childhood play, none matches the sheer heart-ripping tension of volleyball, where forces of incredible control work against equal forces of desire. Never have those who want to win so badly taken the floor within such a set of regulations, with so powerful officials' domination, as when the girls assume their positions. And it is a bunch of girls, usually, for high school volleyball is women's work. Is this game only deeper training for a world of institutionalized sexism, in which the attempt to win is always made within the context of taboo? Such questions to ask of sport! But such a sport of pure tension! And such a sport of pure tension to be woman!

8

Letter

*S*oon after our third child, John III, was born, we began looking for a larger house. It was obvious that two girls fast approaching their teenage years were on the verge of bursting a shared room. Their mental sparks were more of a danger to the household than their burgeoning supply of outgrown and discarded toys. And besides, Jena's arm had outgrown the backyard and Cindy's words needed their own cocoon of walls from which to reverberate, compete with one another and rearrange themselves before emerging to force their way into the world's consciousness. So we turned to the classified ads, real estate section, and began to look. Four years later we found, and bought, four bedrooms with a white-football yard, which we could also almost afford.

During the years we searched, we were inside at least one, and usually several, pieces of property each week. I only remember one of these houses, and that one not because of its floor plan or decor, but rather because of a poem that the out-of-town husband had left for the stay-at-home wife, who in turn had left it taped to the window above the kitchen sink. That the writing revealed a romantic relationship of which the two were proud was, to me, secondary. Instead, I was struck by the power of a written communication left behind for a member of one's immediate family. Believe this: When we live with people, we come to talk to them in the paralanguage of our respective roles; we repeat things just to hear the sound of each other's voices, in the process reassuring ourselves of the family coherence. The written word escapes these acquired restrictions. When those close to us speak in a medium other than the familiar tone of voice, we listen intently. Having seen a poem taped to a window, I've always held the written note in reserve for times I knew that spoken words would be ineffective.

Just such a day came, of course, when I felt I had to write Jena a letter about sports. She had been sick, missed some practices, and faced the possibility of either not playing in a junior varsity volleyball game in a town called Beatrice, or perhaps worse yet, of playing with her teammates knowing she'd missed practice, the one act sure to bench any of them. Her presence on the court would tell the rest of the team that she was considered indispensable, a message she would just as soon leave unsaid. When a game requires the intricate cooperation of volleyball, everyone's mind must be free of the nagging thoughts preferential treatment can send coursing through a group of humans. You don't have to be on varsity to figure that out. She pondered her predicament late into the night, concluding that one solution would be to hold herself out of the game regardless of her coach's wishes. That's when I began composing a letter.

As starting material, I chose some words that had, over twenty years earlier, made more of an impression on me than those of the collected faculty of the University of Oklahoma. I had been a mediocre performer on a somewhat better than average swimming team. I could still, at the age of forty, describe the value of this experience by standing in the shallow end, telling middle-aged friends sprawled in their deck chairs, "like to see everything I learned in college in the next ten minutes?" That assessment was not quite fair, or true. I could also remember why I went chasing dark lines through cold water. The reason was expressed in twenty-three words by an American army general:

Jena,

> *"Upon the fields of friendly strife*
> *are sown the seeds*
> *that, upon other fields, on other days*
> *will bear the fruits of victory."*
> DOUGLAS MACARTHUR

I may have told you one time about a wrinkled piece of paper with MacArthur's quote thumbtacked to the bulletin board near the University of Oklahoma swimming pool. I read that passage every day for four years as I went into the pool and again as I left. Thinking back on all the years of learning to deal with competition, victory, defeat, and the development of my own potential, MacArthur's words stand out as one of the highlights of my college career. He was talking about the athletic programs at West Point when he made those comments, but they are equally applicable today to the situation at East High.

You have always been an extremely "coachable" kid. That is one of your strengths and the basis for your excellence in team sports. You've always done your share and more to bring the team to victory. You are dignified no matter what the outcome, saving your frustrations over a loss for the privacy of your own family, smiling and congratulating your teammates and opponents when you win. Your individual skills, however, have helped bring the self-esteem that accompanies victory

time and time again to those who might not have otherwise had it. You may not be the best in the world, but
you are damn good at what you do and your concentration, coordination, individual efforts, and sense of the
flow of action truly do alter the whole game when you
take the floor.

But now it's time for a biology lesson. The human
being is a wonderful but highly social species. Individ-
ually we produce the finest art, music, scientific ideas,
inventions, and literature. Collectively we are capable
of generating war and strife beyond your wildest imagination. As a group we often fear or hate the rebel, the
explorer, the one who is different in some way, but then
we consume the new ideas just such people provide.
There is a possible explanation for this: In nature, individuals who are different and strong can either replace
the ones who already occupy the species' niche, or
sometimes open up new environments. Individuals
who are different and who are weak either die or are
killed by predators. You are different from the rest in
that your talents are exceptional, especially for a frail-
looking little girl. My purpose in writing this letter is to
encourage you to also be among the strong.

You are now "sowing the seeds that upon other fields
. . ." through schooling, athletics, and music. But when
you willingly give up an opportunity to test your skills,
just to make others happy, then you are poisoning those
seeds. It seems so easy to make other people happy by
being cooperative and nice. But when "cooperative"
and "nice" mean giving up your personal challenge,
then the "fruits of victory" in later years will become
shriveled, drilled with bugs, and infertile.

You have always accepted your coaches' decisions
and we, as parents, have not often interfered. If your
coach decides, for whatever reason, that you won't play
tomorrow, then I know you will accept that decision
calmly and be an enthusiastic supporter of your team's

efforts at Beatrice. On the other hand, if your coach decides you can and will play, then you are faced with the mental test that so often accompanies physical competition. If you decide to hold yourself out just to soothe the feelings of teammates whose win/loss record is in part due to your special skills, then you will suffer an injury just as serious as a sprained ankle. You are strong enough to recover from some of those kinds of injuries. But you are also strong enough to resist them before they happen. The responsibilities of talented people are, first, to develop their abilities, and secondly, to use them for the benefit of a society that doesn't know whether it wants them or not. For history is clear on one point: Regardless of what society thinks it should have, it needs talent today like never before.

If you decide not to play at Beatrice, do so with a clear understanding of what it is you are doing, and more importantly, why you are doing it. Not playing might be, in fact, a fine contribution to your team, if your teammates' dedication is kindled by their increased chances to play while you're on the bench. But that is a short-term effect. Don't let the group keep you down for long, Jena, because it will be the ultimate loser. And don't keep your talent under wraps to make others happy too often, for you will then join them as an ultimate loser.

Dad

I typed the letter in the darkness of very early morning and left it at her breakfast place in the kitchen before I went to work, still in the dark. There is no love lost between Beatrice, a town forty miles away, and East High, even at the junior varsity level. I don't remember the results of the game, but I do remember that she played.

9

Theory of Science

I arrive at a midseason junior varsity tournament. Parents have agreed to sell tickets. No publicity can be expected from this madness, no glory, nothing but a boyfriend's support, a touch of confidence to help try for next year's varsity, and a coach's musing over the success of the farm system. Plus a lot of screaming. Tournament volleyball requires screaming. East High becomes an abstract expressionist play with great swashes of clashing color moving past one another as teams search for their dressing rooms, color-coded parents move in knots to find their bleachers, and straggles of matching cheerleaders stream, like foraging ants, from the concession window. Being here is a pleasure: total relaxation, isolation from the meaningless struggles at the office, and best of all, no personal interest. Varsity has detail at reserve tournaments; Jena, her JV days long behind her, is a line judge. We have a chance to talk about the matches between games, compare notes on players, strategy, officials, coaching philosophies, kids we used to know.

One of the latter is a star. Religion has sent this one to a small parochial school in the city and their varsity gets to play in large school reserve tourneys. Collapsed one evening after practice, Jena throws war and murder on the floor, flips quickly past typical sports journalism in a college town that boasts major football, and searches the corners of the sports section's second page. In smaller letters and shorter paragraphs than next year's baseball trades, a tiny parochial school's volleyball team gets its disproportionate share of ink. Her friend's name is there. The Crusaders have won again. They'll easily work their way into the finals of this tournament. Jena finds herself calling lines on their serves. I'm interested; decide to watch how these two young women, former Angels teammates now gone separate ways, handle their respective roles. Jena is cast as an official, the other girl as a standout player on the favored team. Two people, once thrown together working toward a common goal, now find themselves seeing each other, through athletics, with a different perspective. I sense some potential observations on biology coming from this situation. The insight into human nature, however, comes not from the two Angels who handle their tasks with consummate grace, but from a guy in the stands.

The father behind me is blessed with a champion voice. His child among the blue and gold plays against the Crusaders who will this day demolish their opposition. The man knows every team member by name. You sense they are all his. He is what you'd call a "sports fan." He would play himself if he could, but he can't, so he calls the game from the stands. In his mind are the strings and out on the floor, the puppets. He can anticipate where they need to be and how they need to play the hit. But he can't pull the strings. He curses them, warns them, berates them, lauds them. His voice has a special quality. It cuts through the screaming, the whistles, the bands. His girls must be the only six in the gym who are unable to hear him. They are getting cleaned.

I mentally review CPR. In what condition is this man?

He does not, cannot, know what he is yelling or what effect he is having on those around him. If confronted with his behavior he would deny it. I sense he does this routinely. He is an embarrassment—disheveled, baggy-eyed, red-faced. Side out; he slams his hand on the bleachers and the shot zings through the screaming gym. Ace spike; he stomps his foot and a thousand butts feel the shock. Ace serve; do I call an ambulance or pull my collar up around my neck? He is out of control. Can he be helped? Does he want to be helped? What kind of help would it be? Is there a halfway house for volleyball fathers?

My eyes wander over the crowd. Mothers are well-dressed, manicured, perfectly made-up, almost as if for church instead of an afternoon in a smelly gym. There is a focused heat on their faces, anticipation in their tarsier eyes. I imagine them in slow motion floating from the stands, executing the diving saves, rolls, bumps, ace spikes. Every shoe, skirt, blouse, neck scarf, watchband, contact lens, is a combination of school colors. The fathers rise slowly to clap. No place else could that sport coat, those socks, be worn except to a game. This is the face of my country: attorneys, dentists, college professors gone bonkers over fifteen points and six girls. Consult the Yellow Pages. America is addicted to athletics.

With that conclusion, order begins to emerge, and with order, a reason for being here on this "wasted" afternoon. Preoccupation with any activity can destroy our ability to interact smoothly in a variety of required situations. Addiction to sports can shape not only the value systems of educated adults but also youth's perception of the present and future. My mind generates questions according to the rhythm of play. Side out; the addiction I'm seeing, does it have a genetic basis, and a negative effect on society, or am I making far too much out of a girls' game? Ace spike;

should all this attention to sports inspire a more serious look at athletics as a meaningful social learning activity? Substitution; is there a theory to explain what is happening in this gym? Ace serve; if so, might Howard Cosell be vindicated after all? Game. Match. I tense waiting for what this father is going to say to the sweaty girl who slowly climbs the bleachers toward him.

The man is talking to his daughter as Jena takes the same bleacher seats two at a time and joins me. We sit in the calm and talk about the Crusaders, their futures and individual styles. Then I ask if she could hear this guy from out on the court. The grin starts with raised eyebrows. Certainly she's heard and passed judgment. Then we listen. Behind us the man is consoling the girl. His voice is soft, gentle, resigned, patient. She played well, did her best. There'll be another day. Something is going on here that I don't quite understand. Was it not so important after all that she win, only that she try with all her forces to win? Is it not such a tragedy that she lost, because within a week she'll be on the court again? Has she fulfilled her role by providing him the opportunity to act this way? In a few minutes the father and his daughter will begin the lonely drive home. I try to imagine their conversation. It is an unsettling exercise. Could it be in fact true that regardless of what the media try to lead us to believe, it is more important to play than to win? As usual, in the face of monumental questions a philosopher provides the answers. His name is Thomas Kuhn and I turn, of all places, to his theories of science.

Kuhn is a thinker whose work Jena will read the next year as a college freshman, one who spoke once of scientific revolutions, whose analysis of the way we gain understanding is now a common tool of art critics, and who, in a high school gym now filling with the next batch of clashing teams, school-colored parents and wound-up cheerleaders, lets us make sense out of what was before nonsense. Kuhn's commentary on the human race is this: We are captivated by puzzles. Furthermore, our intellectual environment defines the legitimate problems and the range of solutions; that is, the context within which we try to solve life puzzles. This context is called a paradigm. Whistles announce the next semifinal match. Twelve girls take the floor to try, publicly, to solve a puzzle. The screaming begins. Echos bounce from the paradigm's steel rafters.

Jena takes her place along the back line to watch, in total calmness for a change, a white sphere hurtling toward her. The floor is a maze of marks. Volleyball lines intersect with full court basketball lines which intersect with two perpendicular basketball courts, their free throw lanes and circles. A thousand people ignore everything except the volleyball court; that is part of the social contract on this day. The pregame ritual writes the contract as surely as the net strains all other concerns from the atmosphere. The uniforms are on volleyball players anywhere in the world. The dress of coaches, if they are women, is volleyball fashion. The players themselves radiate the game; they are of a certain build, with certain pregame movements. They will be totally different people when basketball season starts. The referees can belong only to this game. One can tell what they look for by the focus of their attention. All have come to this place to solve a puzzle, to see who is best able to solve this puzzle, and to force a solution from within a given paradigm. Today, here, in this place, that is the definition of "volleyball."

And who are the people I've come to watch, including parents and the "fans" who are as entertaining as the players? They are people who have invested months and years of planning, physical labor, and consideration of alternatives, in order to solve a puzzle. Or, they are people who have come to watch the attempts at solution. The puzzle is defined by a set of rules no less clear than the white paint that shines against the amber wood where Jena rests her molded shoes. Thomas Kuhn revealed how the whole life of an individual scientist can be consumed by a puzzle. Sport, however, no matter what the level, shows how society can become equally mesmerized by a problem. Volleyball, with its plethora of regulations, converts the crowd into the mental equivalent of an individual, at least in part, for an afternoon. By silent agreement, everyone who's come to East High seeks an answer to the question: By what means can a game be won? A victory will demonstrate a solution. Losers will vow that on another day the puzzle will have another solution. I find myself wondering if Thomas Kuhn ever did time in high school gyms.

On the way home, in the car with her father out west of town, the girl listens, watches the golden treeline mark a river, reads the road signs that name the environment from which she must carve her future, the small towns and farms that shape her ideas. The two are talking ball after a humiliating defeat. They talk of next week, of Districts, of next year, of basketball season, of disappointments, victory, schoolwork, the harvest. She has tried her best, and he is proud of her. He would be proud if the loss had been twice as humiliating, had she tried as hard. They don't discuss "character." They've been blitzed by the Crusaders and don't need a morality lesson about strength through adversity. They have what they need. It is unspoken though easily recognized. No one knows better than a teenage girl who turns silent, gazes out over the corn stubble, and softly wipes the tears that run down her face, that a major puzzle, established within the context of a game, could be solved, at least by someone else.

There beside the white line stands our daughter. Her face reveals her own questions: Do my life puzzles have such clear solutions? Side out; where should I go to college? Ace spike; those super running backs I see on television, some of them are only a year older than I am; how could they have gone so far so fast? Ace serve; what should I choose to be? Signalling a point, her hands press the imaginary ball upon the floor inside the white rectangle. Substitution; how do I know at the age of eighteen that my decisions are the right ones? I don't. Probably nobody knows how to make life decisions at age eighteen. Point; so what do I do? Game. Match. Screaming and leaping. I guess I become a solver of puzzles.

Some time during the months that follow she will begin a letter "Dear Coach ————. . ." The letter will go to several colleges and universities. It will briefly summarize her achievements on the volleyball and basketball courts and in the classroom. From her perspective they are considerable. She feels that anyone worth playing for should recognize them easily, unlike some who write for newspapers. The paper mentions "varied offense." Jena sees her name. Another story reads "full court press" and "went into a stall with four minutes left." Jena sees her name. She is not naïve about the matter of playing beyond high school; a little more glory might open a door, extend her future with games. Her letter suggests to people who solve puzzles with humans that she may be able to help.

But she cannot escape the truth. "I rank twenty-seventh in a class of three hundred eighty and have taken calculus, physics, chemistry, zoology, and four years of French." With that statement one eighteen-year-old's life puzzle becomes considerably more complex, for all she's ever really wanted to do is play ball. In a few months she'll stand where thousands have stood before, upon the East High stage in cap and gown, shaking hands with the principal, clasping a diploma. Her transcript would get her into a thousand colleges, her talents into a hundred careers, none of which seem to be calling. Instead, the future looks to be filled with grown-up obligations, not the games that have been her identity. She can defer a life decision if she can just convince someone to give her a chance. But the words "setter" and "guard" leap out from her lines. Every coach in the world can read through those words. She might as well have laid it on the table: I have tried so hard to grow, Coach ———, but I am still just five feet three.

And with that equipment in a year she'll take on the giant Thomas Kuhn. If she can't handle his published thoughts, and others equally as revolutionary, she'll go on playing life games on court after court, in one gym after another. Even at this age she bears the pro-jock burden— memories a succession of buildings, places, eating out; victory a transient thrill; loss a liar who claims there'll be no tomorrow; and always, out beyond the white lines on amber floors, that blurred vision of a world where people do real things, work, make money, read books. To the crowds she gives her time, talents, ballet, and an internal fire that just wants to play ball, and then reads about her accomplishments in paragraphs smaller than the obituaries. If she masters all that Thomas Kuhn has to offer, his insights will be hers; the power of his ideas bent to a million puzzles will guide the hand that sends a sphere upon its lonely way. What is now the world will become her court.

Is there life after high school ball? Yes, if games have been shown to be what they indeed are—problems to be solved. Has she only been playing ball? No. Someone has allowed her, encouraged her, and helped her to join a fray. That someone has confronted a puzzle whose solution requires a grand synthesis of talent identification and selection, conditioning, teaching of techniques and co-ordination, choreography, medical care and analysis, psychological counseling, administration and public relations. If that someone has done these things successfully for enough months or years, then he or she gets to do them under pressure in a situation that places a premium on the movements and mental states of girls. That person will take our daughter and try to accomplish at breakneck speed what I, as a professional scientist, try to do lei-surely over the course of a year—solve problems.

Back on the court are animals, members of the species *Homo sapiens.* They move and crouch and take positions, hearts pounding, faces tense, their spewing hormones sending shivers through their skin. They challenge the en-emy band. Innovation operates at several speeds now, from the months in practice to milliseconds on the court as the sphere comes slammed, trajectories are calculated, antici-pated, met. They will fight until the scoreboard declares the death of hope. Of all the characteristics that distin-guish the competing bands from other species the most spectacular is the driving curiosity which seeks to explain, control, use and manipulate the environment summarized in one word—volleyball. Such control, however, is usually a coach's job.

In the break between games, Jena's coach walks casu-ally in, steps over to speak to her, and sizes up the match. It is a tiny version of the eternal mystery whose answers are known only to those who play and those who teach. What do coaches and players say to one another? Who knows; you just have to be there. But at some time or another over the last few months, this coach has said something that changed the behavior of a group of young women. On this day he will watch for a while, seeing things no one else can see. Movements, sequences of events, techniques, substitutions, will all have a unique meaning for him. Months later that meaning may surface as a new idea. He will then set out to teach this concept. In the process he will also, in a decidedly human decision, perhaps made and carried out subconsciously, try to teach the ability to use his new idea, or not use it, as the occasion demands. This coach does not seem to be a particularly driven person. He is calm, dignified, and sets standards for professionalism at his level. He finds some way to enjoy victory with class ("It doesn't get any better than this!") and he never fails to gather his players around for a final word, win or lose. But he, and the others like him, are the source of the new.

I, a teacher in another kind of game, watch this one with his pupil. By the stir of things there will be action soon. He melts into the stands. I review what this man regularly accomplishes. He demands of himself that anyone who comes to play improve or feel as if she's improved, feel that individual dignity and personal worth are not diminished by a team effort, that a mistake or loss is not as serious as lack of effort, that a creative contribution is endorsed, that the activity is of more value than the product. He demands of himself that his players become acquisitors and integrators. He handles tears of frustration and tears of joy and tears of personal disappointment as teammates leap and scream with crazy victory, all with grace. He wakes in the morning after a stunning win to find that those in whom he's invested superhuman patience have strung his shrubbery with toilet paper. Thomas Kuhn would be proud of this person who seems to have learned how to solve, regularly, an enormous and challenging puzzle called volleyball.

10

Coach of the Year

You would never be able to see it on his face had you not, in times past, tried with all your might to beat someone and failed. It is not always a pleasant look, that of victory over one's own emotions. Deep within is an untamed desire to win, to have won. That desire gnaws away at his insides. On the surface he appears to have conquered it. His girls may leap, hug, scream; he smiles. On another night his girls cry, or slump on the bench. He shakes hands with the winner. Jena seethes, smolders, wipes her face, glares at the team she's just congratulated, while her body's physiology re-adjusts itself, hormones are dissipated, visceral circulation restored, and her mind wonders what it will be like tomorrow, if there is a tomorrow. She's pushed beyond the limits and lost; she can see the price he's paying for his victory over defeat. The price is a rationalization: All you want to do is win, but the best you can do is win more than you lose. And to do that, you must do the hardest thing of all—you must teach.

Somehow on this night the two don't seem connected. To know you've taught well just doesn't erase the loss. Tomorrow, maybe, or next week or the week after, when we look back on our year, we'll say we had fun, learned some ball, learned something of ourselves and how to work as a team, saw effort transform itself into progress. But tonight we just wanted to win! Oh God how we wanted to win! Like we did the last two times we played that team, with a hard fought, exciting, down-to-the-wire, gut-wrenching win. Why couldn't we win, so he could say "it doesn't get any better than this" and Jena could come home and we could watch the confidence creep over her as she curls up in a chair and closes her eyes? Instead we have game films. A reporter is busy scribbling, looking at a notebook. The camera, however, shows something else.

"You can tell what kind of questions he's asking by the look on Mr. Oehlerking's face," says Jena. The picture also tells us the reporter has never coached, never explained away a loss, restrained his pleasure over victory, converted the intangible potential of desire into the solid reality of a score and a trophy. "Mr. O." is staring past the man. What does a losing coach say to a reporter? We read something in the paper but it may not be at all what was said, or meant. What does a losing coach say to himself?

The players know. They know how to act when desires go inward. Jena's learned well. She smiles, nods cheerfully, is the first to congratulate an opposing coach, and seek out certain players, not the ones who get the glory, the spikers and high-scoring centers and forwards, but the guards and setters, to tell them they had a good game. Then she goes home and fights her feelings. Sometimes it goes away by morning; sometimes it lingers for days, weeks. Then the seeds begin to sprout, slowly, almost pushing to the surface between the boards. She looks back. She is alive, healthy;

her grades are good; her friends still call. And at season's end, she hears again the words she's heard so often, from Coach of the Year.

"We relaxed and had a lot of fun, played a lot of ball, learned some things, made some progress . . ." they drone on at any year's awards banquet. We'd talked a great deal about volleyball when she failed to make varsity as a sophomore. I sat in the stands at reserve games and fumed: She's good enough to play varsity. So were some others, it turned out, and they were older, more experienced at a game far more complex than any of us knew. He'd had his priorities straight. Determination and self-confidence slip away on the bench but grow on the court. It was almost as if he'd played this game so many times there were no surprises. Three years earlier he'd wanted her out on the floor every possible minute, so he sent her to the reserves. Then, three years later, her career as a varsity starter at an end, he stands and smiles, says he'll be happy to help her find a place to play in college if he can.

We didn't have to be told that. We've watched him work and know it's already been done. We sit one evening in the East High cafeteria chewing on blue and white mints after a potluck, making small talk with cheerleaders. She gets her second varsity letter and takes her seat. Parents applaud. Back at the table we look at her final stat sheet. It tells a story. His words have had the desired effect: Try to improve, just improve, every day, every game. Do better than your last performance, just a little better. The short speech, heard so many times it's memorized, brings to mind the mathematical equations of growth. Our reaction to these laws is a product of the ideas by which they're surrounded at the moment. When it comes to debt, or weapons, or populations, we turn away and hide our eyes; but when our bank account's involved, we want steady growth. Nor are we frightened by the equations when we see them in operation on the court. He understands the higher math. Have fun, play a little volleyball, learn some things . . . improve every day. You can't improve every day without growing exponentially in your skills and ability. The place you start from is yesterday's improvement. He coaches by the laws of compound interest.

Growth is a process widely discussed but rarely understood, in its full impact, by those who use its name. To grow is to increase—elementary. To grow for any significant length of time, or at any noticeable rate, is to double in capacity, or bulk, in an unbelievably short period. Improve your skills only 5 percent every workout and after two weeks you're twice, and by season's end eight times, the player you were on the first day of practice. A coach who could produce such growth would have a contender every year. A player who learns to grow, and not just at ball games, has tapped a secret of untold power over failure and disappointment.

The score runs on, 7–3, 8–3, 9–3; East is on a roll, opening round, state tournament, defending champion, frustrated and dominated in the first game, fighting to come back in the second, make it to the semifinals. He substitutes. This isn't supposed to happen. The opposing coach is supposed to substitute, save a time out, break the rhythm of service and of the digital scoreboard notching relentlessly toward fifteen. But he substitutes. A senior stands outside the line, her hands palm to palm with a junior. The sign of the cross is made. There is movement but the rhythm is broken. I sit crammed in the high-rise seats, seeing exactly what I want to see of a game about which I know nothing. Arrogant, aggressive, I take the full privileges of a fan, the mind set you can buy for three dollars and a box of popcorn. You call it how you see it; but if nothing else is accomplished this year, seniors will play in the state tournament.

10–4, 10–5, 10–6. Her career is ending here tonight second by second right in front of our eyes. Small town is cramming it back down East's throat, loving it. This is the last time we'll watch her meet the white sphere in blue uniform, the symbol for all those things that mean so much in years that never come again. 10–7; set the ball, Jena, let us watch for one more time. 10–8; jump your tiny body, dink it on their slammer's toes. 10–9; bump their hotdog's wobbly serve, place it in that perfect spot. 10–10. The momentum shifts beyond the point of recovery. East goes over in two games. Afterwards I bend way over the guard rail, reaching down to grab a sweaty head of tousled blond.

"You've got nothing to be ashamed of."

She nods, understanding. There is nothing for anybody to be ashamed of tonight, or last week or last month or last however long those times have gone while she's just run, and tipped a ball, and afterwards stood tall and proud of five feet three that's all there is.

He'd sensed it coming. He saw something out there tonight way in advance of the rest of us. Whatever he saw, it must have sent some kind of a chill through him, because he acted, sent in a senior for her last game. When it was over, many things could be said. To a reporter who asks what does it feel like for a defending state champion to lose in the first round; what went wrong? To a parent who says you've beat them twice before this season; what went wrong? To his players: We couldn't seem to keep the lead; what went wrong? To himself: They've worked, and tried their best to learn, and given me their all, and no matter what the score, came out better than they went in, played at games they loved, and tasted the best. They couldn't completely erase the frustration, but not one sat on the bench and watched everything slip away to midnight saying "is that all there is?" I've tried to teach; they've won more than they've lost. They all improved a little bit every day. Nothing went wrong.

11

Practice

*A*h, don't pass the ball to the midget inside!"

Seems like good advice; logical. Everybody nods, a few smile. This is controlled, ritualized play: scrimmage, or "scrummage," affectionately, almost in the same tone of voice used for "medicine ball" and "suicides." These words carry the same indescribable sense of the personal as do "practice sweats," laundered for once, folded just as affectionately by a mother who puts the still-hot reversible shirt to her face and smells the combination of cleanness, fabric softener, and daughter. The crowds, the band, the whistles, the newspaper stories, all fade, now, in the presence of the reversible heavy T-shirt. It is the symbol for the real meaning of having made the team: You get to practice with the varsity. It is also a hallowed possession, worn only on special occasions—every day from October through March.

"She misses her sports. When you've practiced every day since you were this high, then it's over, you know there's a void. . . ."

This is party conversation, small talk, on the surface, a mother answering the usual question about her daughter:

How does Julie like college? The woman reviews Julie's high school career, some of the disappointments, highlights, the speed with which it all, suddenly, came to an end, while we sit and wonder how we'll answer the same question about Jena in the future. The mother doesn't mention specific games, just generalizes about having "done well" one year, not so well another. But then we are all silent. The adults around this conversation sit thinking, sharing the look back into events which structured our only lives, only chances on earth to see our children grow up. Shared feelings bind us in the same way practice bound the events of Julie's life, and still tie Jena's, into a context, gave it texture, filled the mind with a daily dose of vision quest. Such a load to lay on practice!

Someone mentions, finally, the organization symbolized by the reversible T-shirt. In the drone of this conversation, the mind wanders, thinking of the writer with his chattering Selectric; the musician with her scales, five, six hours of finger exercises, she says with a smile, every day; the artist with his pencil moving in the privacy of a time he seals against the crowd that swirls in and out of the coffee shop; the scientist lost in journal page after journal page, turning, absorbing; the pheromonic trail laid by previous decisions taking all of them into the society of their practice, merging their pasts, their futures, leading them with their own ideas, saying as can no other entity: You are ————. Such a high and mighty attribute for such a lowly, sweaty activity as, well, put bluntly, practice!

"Ah, some of you were late for practice the last two days. I said 8:30; I expect you here on the floor at 8:30, not dragging in at 8:32, 8:33. So, we're going to run some laps. This is called 'peer pressure.' Maybe some of you can get the others to get in here on time." Whistle. Sheepish grins creep up and down the line. They know what it is; they know he knows they know what it is: peer pressure. The silent pounding of shoes bounces off the beams of an empty gym, down court, returning louder, down court into the distance, the line getting ragged; some are faster than others. Still they cannot erase the grins. Later in the car they will complain, quite unconvincingly. Someone was late for practice. Jena will tell who it is, again unconvinced it was important enough to run laps, or that laps are much punishment anyway. The pounding continues, mixed now with breathing, mixtures of sounds you never hear in games. Punishment ends. They lean, some sucking air, against the wall; others walk slowly, shaking their ankles, circling, breathing in great gulps. Outside half the city is without electricity. Two days ago the ice swept in, its unmerciful weight downing trees across the lines. Willows seem to be the most fragile; they always break under pressure. Crews have been working around the clock. Winter sports. And a forward named Cathy was two minutes late to, yes, practice.

"Ah, okay; medicine ball." Again the pounding. Pairs start down the floor with no hesitation. They are also established by some forces to which each person is alert, forces not at work in games, where circumstances dictate action. In paired drills, some electricity of shared ideals, experiences, attitudes, bind them in units of their own choosing. The rhythm of paired drill is described by any machine that will generate a wave—a computer, a transmitter, hooked to a screen upon which the never-ending ups and downs show only changes in amplitude, or frequency, that mirror tired muscles. Peggy and Jena set the speed to the far end of the court and return, then step aside; the medicine ball stays in its oscillating orbit, controlled now by

Julie and Amy, temporary possessors of the sphere which generates succeeding waves; Peggy and Jena oscillate beside Julie and Amy, then all shift one energy level. The ball is alive; its tracks above the court go back and forth in compressed loops where pairs of drill-friends run and throw the heavy lump then pass it to the next in line. Janet and Kathy up and down, up and down, now Julie and Amy oscillate with basketball, a lower energy level, a lighter electron, till Peggy and Jena start the cycle over again. Medicine ball, they hope, will generate waves of other things: Frail arms will, next Tuesday, hold that pass flung the length of the court on the fast break. Medicine ball generates waves of hope. In practice.

"Ah, okay, we're going to scrimmage six quarters. Jena, Tami, Julie, Peggy, Janet . . . Amy, the other Julie, Cathy, Karen . . ." No fanfare, no excitement, no screaming comes with scrimmage, only the hushed sounds of breathing, T-shirts being pulled off and reversed to separate the teams by color, shoes squeaking on the polished boards, the metallic rattle of the clock board being plugged in, the student manager dragging her chair over to the side. "First two quarters . . ." and his voice trails off into which offense goes against which defense for how long. Scrimmage has a smoothness never seen in games, derived, perhaps, from the closeness of the players, from the agreement that certain knowledge has to be suppressed before the practice is functional. It's not fair to steal in scrimmage since you know where the ball is meant to go. We are supposed to be beyond that, well into the mental realm where patterns are run until they are run unconsciously, where individual moves are moved until a repertoire is built, and from which they can then be drawn without thinking.

But above all, it is the sound of scrimmage which sets it

apart from the game. Everything echoes: the whistles, the breathing, the soles squealing "popout" or "triple pick" as the defense shifts to man-to-man, the pounding, always the pounding, of basketball, the hypnotic heartbeat pounding, pounding into the rafters, pounding in the ears out on icy streets, home in the darkness of the early hours as traffic throws its light through bedroom windows; the body pumps its own life with the pounding of a basketball in an empty gym. Once in a while someone shouts. "Nice shot!" . . . nice shot . . . nice shot. Then something suddenly happens that can never happen in a game: seminar. The clock is stopped and discussion follows. Voices are academic, the deeper tones alternating with higher queries, suggestions. All echo. End of class. White out of bounds on the side.

You hear about the techniques for teaching the fine art of making free throws, the advice of those who do it well, of those who teach players to do it well. "I heard they . . ." and the voice trails off into some wild tale of a coach who brings his girls into the gym for blindfolded free throw practice, late at night, then buys them steak dinners if they make twenty-five in a row, blindfolded. Six baskets around the gym are lowered. Drill pairs disperse to the far corners, one to watch, one to shoot, then the other to watch and the other to shoot, twelve versions of what must occur, the exact set of motions that must accompany a free throw, before providence will place the ball into the holy ring. Nothing is free about a free throw. Instead, you pay for it with the sudden loneliness of the individual against her own preoccupations in a sport where nothing, except a free throw, is intended to involve just one person. She must now do something on her own: make a basket with her friend watching. And on Thursday night, if she's "lucky," make a basket with the world watching, half of it holding its breath in hope, half of it willing her failure, jeering, yelling, "Miss it! You're gonna miss it! Hey! Hey!" Try as he might, there is no way for a coach to duplicate this circumstance in practice. "Free throws." Enough said. Pairs move as far apart as they can within a single gym. Even this dispersal is symbolic: The amoeba breaks into its molecules for a token homage to the individual. Territories become large. Afterwards comes relief. Now, with that little incongruity out of our system, we'll run.

At the end of it, one by one they move slowly to the door, form long and patient lines at the water fountain, the look of practice on their faces, then slip into the long hall to the girls' dressing room. Winter sun casts shadows down a polished hall. The walls are lined with showcases, their frozen gilded guards forever in the act of layup, nets draped like spider webs behind the glass, faces of the years: coaches gone, players gone, forever watching the procession creaking its straggling way to the lockers, binding into some kind of history the shared pain of practice. "Do as well as we did!" The shout echoes through a vacant school. "Go!" She turns and looks into the showcase. There is a glare, a reflection on the window, on the glass. "Go!" . . . "Go!" She leans her body against the crash bars on the outside door and pushes. Winter is waiting, wind driving snow. She holds her precious shoes beneath her coat. The empty gym waits.

12

Time-outs

*L*ife patterns are largely expressions of one's measure of time. A chemist can think in terms of the microseconds it takes for atoms to collide. Paleontologists compress the events of a hundred sixty million years into a single word—Mesozoic—then conjure up a world of dinosaurs on drifting continents. And to a physicist, multibillion-year pulsations of the universe are as real as the house next door. In the city, people look at their watches, then scurry a little faster, or sit rapping on a steering wheel as high in a church steeple another hour is marked by chimes. But on the court, time starts with a whistle and ends with a buzzer. Everything outside those symbolic brackets is time-out.

Deep into the night she sits at the word processor. Two things happen in the next forty-eight hours. First, district volleyball begins with the opening match against a team that makes few unforced errors, has handed East one of its four losses this season, and has played to the wire for every point. If East wins, it gets to play a team that's produced two of the remaining three losses, one of which was a two-pointer in the third game. If East wins again, it goes to the state tournament. Second, a major paper is due, an analysis of a state agency. Beside her are her notes, research from the local newspaper library, and a calculator. By the grace of God the next forty-eight hours does not include an exam in calculus or French. But a new, virulent head cold and the attendant splitting sinus headache compete with assignments for her attention. Upstairs no one is awake. Periodically she saves text onto a diskette. Some time later she hits CTRL-P, answers NP, and the dot printer spits into action. Her shoulders sag; her eyes burn and she rubs them. All she wants to do is play ball.

A singing wind drives snow against the bricks. Even the weather signals competition for her time—soon there'll be a holiday, and with it travel to the south, where families gather; her parents lived down there when they were young. But a coach will also need her time; holidays bring tournaments along with gifts and decorations. The issue is not challenged directly. The player won't ask to go to grandmother's if the coach will cancel practice, and both will take their separate ways until after Christmas. In the lull she stands before the ancient Spiro burial mounds, reconstructed for all who seek museums to pass the idle hours away from home. Peering through the showcase glass, her mind goes back to a time that, well, put bluntly, no one who makes a religion of the present, can imagine. Human beings, with hands like hers, eyes that could recognize, voices that could cry out, chipped the flint, sewed the skins, twisted reeds and bent them into baskets, had their babies, lived, died, taught one another. There were no cars, no electric lights, no Interstates, no television sets, no computers, no nuclear missiles. Rivers raged. Spirits brought the lightning, visions, meat. There was no time. In the end she asks if we have really made progress. I answer no. Then she asks if we can drive to another town. In that town there lives an uncle. He has the keys to a high school gym. I answer yes.

The mixtures of desires and requirements seem to go back all the years adults have been involved in her life. Postseason basketball tournament memories, from far off big cities, are some of the most incongruous, even surreal, as parents searched for ways to fill the space between semifinal games. In a giant somber building marble-vaulted ceilings echo her footsteps. Her eyes are wide now, darting from wall to wall, stopping, captured momentarily by cricket cages, houses, cricket food and water dishes, elaborate enameled boxes, swords, coins, broken terra cotta horses fading to ibis mummies. The scene shifts to Andy Warhol, Richard Hunt, but she stands finally in front of Steinberg, following the allegory, questioning. Satisfied, she's dragged to the Dark Ages, variations on the theme of Madonna, evil, passion, writhing condemnation. Spanish elegance, Italian eyes, follow her; arrogance and suspicion of a thousand years watch an American girl kill three hours in a strange town. Near the end she finds relief. Remington provides the guts, Bierstadt the glory. The coachable one looks at her watch and calls in her aces. It's time to go play ball.

Spring comes late, if at all, to the northern plains. One day sleet covers new leaves, the next you're searching frantically for shorts buried in some November closet. In late spring, the seriousness of sport in higher paradigms comes with the afternoon mail. A big university runs a summer basketball camp; deposits and reservations are due. But the forms will have to be forwarded because by now she's a

universe away from painted lines and circles, walking the
hills of Jordan country, and listening to the brittle grass
make whispers on her jeans. Everyone touches the baby
owls, but only she holds one up to her face to feel the little
head trembling bleary-eyed against her cheek. I take a picture. She wades in waist-deep for snails. On the prairies
you can always get grasshoppers to feed the biggest toad of
all. Don't worry, a hundred pelicans will spiral on ther-
mals above your head again tomorrow. Drive oh so slowly,
please, the killdeer chicks are on this road. The canoe is
heavy, but it gets you out to wrens. Which is more spectacular, this sunset or the one last evening? She doesn't
care. At four this morning she sits with falling stars. Jena,
it's near the end of June. Cowboy music. I know. Jena, it's
mid-July; camp starts in a week. I guess you're right. Take
me into town to play some hoops?

On the first of several biting, spitting November days, she
stands inside a circle watching two basketballs being
placed upon the floor, one on each "block," a solidly
painted rectangle alongside the lane beneath the basket. A
teammate stands to the side, ready, anticipating.
    "Go!"
    The click of a stopwatch sets her bolting into a dash for
the ball which is then in her hands and into the basket,
then the other ball is in the air and her partner snaps up
the first rebound and lays it back on its block. Again and
again at top speed, pushing, pushing ever faster, she goes
from block to block, ball to ball, layup to layup until click
it's over. Thirty seconds have seemed like thirty years. She
asks herself how many layups from the blocks a person can
do in thirty years. She listens to her own breathing as she
watches a man write down the results of her test, and wonders if a person can be a coach without a clipboard. The

man looks up and nods. Her teammate steps into the circle.

The painted lane beneath the basket rules many actions, depending on the context that happens to surround it. On this afternoon it's a measure of her performance in a series of timed drills. Playing coach in the privacy of her thoughts, she mentally evaluates the rest of her team, in pairs, going through their forced layups from rebounds fielded and placed on the blocks. She decides which ones will earn their places in the starting lineup, wonders when, if ever, in a game she'll do these same moves. She smiles, remembering times someone's laid the ball on the floor, not intentionally, of course, like now, but nevertheless put it there on the blocks free and loose. When you're as close to the floor as she is, you love a loose ball.

The lane changes roles; now it's a space to be negotiated. She stands facing the far end of the court, its backboard a distant pattern against the tile wall above a drinking fountain.

"Go!"

Again the watch sets her into motion, "sliding" across the lane and back, never crossing her feet, again and again, back and forth, for another thirty seconds. Click! He writes in silence; all her skills, her moves, instincts and reflexes, are being translated into numbers. She thinks about the other measured items in her life: money, clothes, miles per hour, scores on history tests, quarters of play, fouls, steals, and assists per game. She turns. On the wall is a board filled with names and numbers—school records. Below the board is a piece of tape marked off in feet and inches. The clock has finally counted out its days and minutes until now there's no time left. Of all the drills she's done this afternoon, a final one remains to remind her of the place she's tried to make for herself. She walks to the wall, reaches as high as she can. The man notes on his clipboard the place her fingers touch the tape. She glares at the wall, then leaps for the sky.

In a few days she gets a written summary and evaluation of her performance in the standing jump, running jump, slides across the lane, layups from the blocks . . . Then the coach hands her several sheets of diagrams, mimeographed numbers and arrows drawn around a lane and a free throw circle. On the page of explanations, the number 1 is said to mean "small guard." She studies the planned moves for number 1 and wonders if they have anything at all to do with reality. Upon the summary sheet is a record of her past, in numbers. Upon the page of diagrams is a vision of the future, again in numbers. She looks at the calendar. The date of their first game is circled. In three weeks it will be time to go play ball.

She sits back on a table, her leg extended straight out, hanging over the edge at midcalf, foot held upwards at a right angle. The person in front of her shakes a spray can, checks the top to make sure it's aimed correctly, then presses to direct the stream of mist over the ankle and foot. Jena watches this ritual with serious attention; what is about to happen in the next few minutes is a critical part of what will happen in the next hour or two. A thin, foamy sheet of plastic is folded around her foot. Then comes the two sounds of tape—being pulled from the roll, and being ripped. A piece encircles her leg right above the ankle; rip. A piece is wound around the ankle; rip. Another goes around the arch of her foot; rip. A piece is laid along the outside of her foot, stretched around her heel, measured along the inside, ripped, and stuck down. Two stirrups go from the lower calf, under her foot, and back up. Figure eights run down one side and in back of her leg, beneath her heel, then up and over to the other side. Everything is tied in place with bands around the ankle and calf. She moves her foot, climbs down off the table, stands on it, thinks, and nods approval. Then she walks barefoot into the dressing room, sits down, puts on a thin sock, then a thick one over it, and finally her shoe. She pulls the laces exactly the right amount, double ties them, then stands to feel the work that's been done. The foot sends no distracting messages to her brain. One ankle is ready to play ball.

She has memorized every feature of this room, every tile, how it was laid straight or crooked, the grain pattern in every wooden bench, the locker numbers, imperfections in the mirrors, the sounds of each blow dryer and shower— she can tell which one is being used without looking. She is also quickly memorizing the writing on a blackboard. Her name is beside a number, but it's not her number; instead it belongs to a girl from another city. She's never seen this girl, never watched her move her feet, assessed her abilities to dribble left- or right-handed, drive to the basket, put her hand in another's face, anticipate the pass, or steal. But she has a description on the dittoed report: good, quick, watch her on the fast break, has trouble getting the ball inside, don't let her set up and shoot.

She studies the rest of the list on the blackboard. Beside each number is the name of one of her teammates. So tonight the girls play man-to-man, at least in the beginning. While all she knows about the other team's numbers come from a sheet of paper and a coach's words, her teammates' names are a different matter. She knows their likes and dislikes, their fears and hopes, the way they play under pressure, or with a minor injury, how easily they're intimidated, or how their concentration can or can't be broken. She knows which ones will always block out, which will have the rebound or else, and how they'll act if they win, or lose, which ones she'd foul if she were playing against them and which ones to avoid fouling because they never miss a free throw. She analyzes the matchups, the game plan so logical, at least on paper. She wonders what the scouting report says about her, what words are written beside her number in the other locker room, or whether she's just an "x" because they're opening with a zone defense and care only that she's a guard, not #34 guard.

She listens carefully to her coach, a young man in his first varsity season. She has total confidence that in a few minutes everyone will do exactly what has been planned. Nobody anticipates being behind five, ten, or even twenty points. Nothing on the blackboard tells what to do if that happens. The muffled sound of the band, the yells in unison, both work their ways through concrete block walls. A student manager comes in and says something to the coach, who turns to his team and claps his hands.

"All right, let's go!"

Standing on the court she gets a look at the number that was beside her name. The person is not what she had imagined. She notes the color of her hair, her size, the look on her face, whether it communicates "smart" or "dumb" or "just plain scared." She studies the wrappings on the other's knee, her brand of shoes, the socks that bulge to reveal a hidden taped ankle. She wonders how long it will take before this one is replaced by a sub, and whether the substitute will be as good, or even better. Subs get no scouting reports. The ref raises his hand, checks the scorer's table and his partner on the floor. It's time to go play ball.

Every day she gets up at seven, is on her way to school thirty minutes later, only to wait. She won't know what was in the mail until three-thirty. The waiting is scheduled—math, French, physics . . . then walk home. April 15 is the magic day. All the videotapes, visits, phone calls, assurances, hopes, focus on the calendar. Income tax returns are items from another universe, but national letters of intent, documents that spell out a chance to play in college, come due on the one hundred fifth day of the year. She flips through the envelopes and picks out one with familiar letterhead. Inside are two multicopy forms. The language on these forms is strange legalese, but it could be Russian and she'd have no trouble translating and knowing where to sign. After all the waiting, the travels and interviews, the comments "if you were just a little taller we'd be interested . . . ," comes a fat envelope with the telltale letterhead. She never hesitates. When the right school and the right coach, just the right distance from home, say "welcome," you grab the opportunity. She signs the letter then looks at the calendar. It's April 15. In six months it will be time for ball.

The final road trip is to North Dakota, on the bus, along with the men's team, to play the powers of the conference. Commercial-type buses have regular-size seats for irregular-size people who take turns lying down in the aisles. Dreary, bleak, beat down, sodden frozen cattle-tramped landscape fades away into black distance, finally to be obliterated by mud spattered on dark windows. Constant shuffling, sometimes explosive cursing from a card game, the hiss of air brakes, short attempts to read, switching of cassettes in Walkmans, vacant stares into passing fields, are punctuated by the folding and unfolding of long arms and legs. The coaches take turns driving. Once in a while the bus meets an oncoming truck with a concussion of air, a rush, as the two hurtling machines pass in the night. She sleeps among giants. At their destination she wakes, looks out at the stores. Old and dirty snow forms a crust over houses. On the streets pedestrians wear heavy parkas. She wonders what kind of people moved here in the beginning.

At a local restaurant they'll be polite, talkative, excited. Their coach sits at one end of a row of tables, seemingly part of the group but always counting minutes, reviewing strategy, thinking through and through a set of human movements until she's convinced they'll occur just as planned, but knowing too that nobody ever choreographed a game, at least completely. A trainer counts calories for twelve others, mentally inventories tape, aspirin, smelling salts. The assistant coach adds bills, pays, circulates. The talk is of classes, television programs, home towns, nothing serious; they've all said these same things a thousand times before.

Visiting teams are as inconspicuous as flying saucers. On the sidewalk to the gym, tall people gaze up at buildings; eyes take in the angles, distribution of windows, niches where the starlings roost; each individual organizes a strange environment in some unique way in order to make it seem like home. Almost involuntarily, they absorb the architecture then reconstruct it to suit themselves. Later they'll see only what they must: backboards, their teammates in or out of position, a swirling pattern of motion. They are all dressed nicely, no jeans; all carry a bag of school colors. They find a heavy metal door, enter, and walk single file along the edge of the court, beside men unloading bags of ice at concession stands, and toward a sign that says "Visitors Locker Room." They've been in rooms with a name like that before. In an hour it will be time to play ball.

The telephone call to a local high school coach was made for one reason, but her question was turned around in an unexpected way. She explained her situation first: I have this regimen of summer exercise, prescriptions for my months ahead. We're so far from home, in the Sandhills where years ago I pitched for the Astros, . . . now I play a different game. I need an inside floor, where the wind doesn't blow, and a backboard with a hoop. Could I get into the high school gym? she asks, then listens for the answer. But when it comes, it's not an answer but another question. Her eyes brighten. Would she be able to coach at his summer basketball camp for middle school girls? They'd be thrilled, he said, out in this part of the country, to have a real college player on their staff. Could she coach? Yes, she says, she can teach.

I'd had car trouble, had to take the old station wagon into town. She'd gone in earlier, in the other car, to her week-long coaching job. After all the years of playing, suddenly it was "Coach Jena." I left the wagon at the garage with a lengthy description of the kind of eccentricities ancient cars can generate in their electrical systems, then walked to the gym. I'd borrow her equally used car for the day then come back to town, pick up the wagon at the garage, etc., etc. . . . all those complexities that seem to plague the American family at some stage in its development. In the gym I sit patiently for a break in the action to tell her of my plan. She is surrounded by girls half her age and half again her size. They break up into pairs—individual offensive/defensive moves drill. There is something vaguely familiar about them all. Then it hits me. They are Jena clones. Their hands, arms, wary stances, foot positions, but mostly their movements, anticipation, and ever-present potential burst of drive around to the basket or open pass, are all hers. Yes, she can teach.

Some afternoon in the future she will close her locker for the last time, walk alongside the vacant court, and casu-ally bounce a basketball on the spring sidewalk through the campus. She'll look out over the parking lots, between the buildings, and down the streets that have become so familiar as a final place to wear that mystical number 34. The months and years to follow carry all the uncertainties they've ever held for billions of humans who've already walked the face of her planet. The striking individuality of a unique life depends as much on these unknowns as on the experiences and genes she alone possesses. But one absolute and given event lies ahead, a shining singularity in the void of unpredictability. No matter what else happens, a day will come when she'll say to a child, as she's said to herself, and some others once said to her: Time-out's over, let's play ball.

13

~

Varsity

*H*e is called John Strain, his surname describing life at
the moment and at many telling moments in the last few
weeks. He is young and tall, as most basketball players are,
so there are no questions about his obvious credentials for
his new job. Besides, his name used to be in the papers a
great deal, back when he played for one of the local colleges. Some people that he played against even in high
school are still around, and they don't look very old either.
None of them look old enough for memories to have faded
into any of the mellowness that surfaces on the downhill
side of life. Strain has on a light brown, three-piece suit;
his other three-piece suit is light blue, cut identically. One
of the guys he used to play against has on black pants and a
black-and-white striped shirt. Parents who know the relationship between the two men, and have watched for the
past hour, can imagine a few flashing moments of history
in which a much younger and thinner John Strain lofts a
final shot over the other's upstretched hands to win a state
championship. But those days are long gone. The ref has
made a very hasty exit from a girls' gym. Coach Strain is

going nowhere. This grown man sits stunned and in tears over a game played by teenage girls.

What does it mean to be on varsity? Looking back, it seems the first year is the educational one, the time when you learn what it means to carry the banner for your school, get your name in the papers, find out what your heroes are all about, see a coach behind the scenes, get told what to do, then sent out on the floor with a push, into the middle of a dogfight, the motion, their uniforms right up close, body contact, hand in your face, elbow in your side, or if you're short, in your eye. Varsity means long, deep philosophical talks with mom and dad after losses. Varsity means you've still got another one to play after a win. Varsity means the highest ups and lowest downs. Let's see, from my first varsity years, one in high school, one in college, what would I tell a kid about varsity?

The forgotten team Coach Strain played for in high school must have whipped up repeatedly on that ref's equally forgotten team. What else could produce the kinds of feelings that must have entered a girls' gym tonight? Few things other than high school games, that's what. Years ago, when they were young, neither had control over their encounter, except for that allowed by talents in a game they both played well. At age eighteen we're no strangers to power derived from skill—even a child can sit down at the piano, hypnotize a recital audience, take a bow, and understand she's held a room full of adults temporarily captive. The power that comes by virtue of position, however, is another matter altogether, especially when one of two former opponents ends up as an official. John Strain will get his name in the papers again in the morning, down in the stats with his girls. They always list a coach's technical fouls in the summaries.

"Marian is a Catholic school," says Jena, "did he have to come off the bench and yell 'Jesus Christ' at the top of his voice?"

"Yes, I think he did." So I pass judgment on the final seconds of a long night when #7-ranked East invades the cloister to take on #2-ranked Marian fifty miles away in the big city. The invaders put Marian into bonus within the first minute of each half. It was all downhill from there. Marian played with seven, against Strain's five, and two of their seven were big guys in striped shirts; that's what Bo, East's other guard, said afterward. Jena said Bo said that right into one of those ref's face.

Varsity is watching your best friend get cut. Back when we all played out on the driveway, nobody got cut, just like that. The first thing that happens is the coach you're supposed to work your guts out for the next five or six months sends your best friend down to play on the reserves. Have you ever watched the reserves? Closely? They try hard; they do their best; most of them will play varsity next year. But their parents, and sometimes grandparents, are the only ones who ever come to watch. The band never plays for the reserve games. Sometimes the concession stand doesn't even open. They hardly ever get their names in the papers. If there's a lot of other sports going on that weekend, they don't even print their summaries. That's what it's like playing on reserves.

But the crowds come to watch varsity, so another thing that happens is that you have to answer to somebody other than yourself and your folks: the fans. They'll analyze your game, give you all kinds of advice, encouragement, clap when you do something great, even if you're a thousand points behind. They'll also decide to go to the guys' game instead of yours. They eat a lot of popcorn. They come down on the floor afterwards and tell Mr. Strain a lot of things but most of them don't know very much about what really went on. The game looks different from down on the floor, compared to up in the stands. But then you don't have to be on varsity to find that out.

No matter how many times she does it, it's still her most beautiful act, the finishing touch on what she does best: steal and run. She steals, picks it up on the run, full court speed with converging behemoths, all collide as she floats heavenward in slow motion moving the ball with her left hand through the traffic and they slash and pound her into the floor and bodies pile into the sickening sound of flesh thrown on tile. The sphere enters the metal ring, kissing the net swish for what should have been her 22nd and 23rd points of a better evening. Angry whistle blows, angry hands spin, the travel, the sneer, the pointing, the strain, the Strain.

"JESUS CHRIST!"

The technical—one of several this season, his first as a varsity coach, in defense of women's honor. The Marian girl makes both shots. They get the ball out of bounds and score on the possession. East loses by three. You're determined not to blame it all on a six-point shift during fifteen seconds of playing time when that fool called Jena for traveling on the layup while those girls beat up on her and her coach came off the bench and . . . So I ask the question I always ask, the next morning, as she sits brooding at the kitchen bar over a gigantic glass of orange juice.

"Was the officiating really that bad?"

Usually when I ask that she tells me the reality of the night before, outlining in detail every foul on every player, how her team got by with such and such and they never called it, how the other team did the same, how it all evened out, bad for bad, good for good.

"Yes, it was."

"I think it's more important for Mr. Strain to come off the bench for you girls than to win."

She gives me the look that says she's having trouble reconciling the same feeling with the frustration of a loss.

"Marian is Catholic. He could have come out there yelling something else besides 'Jesus Christ.'"

"Did you travel?"

"No."

Varsity means you can get emotionally all worked up about a big game. Sometimes that helps, sometimes it doesn't. It's best when the other team is ranked up high and maybe has some super player that everybody knows can be a real snot. Then it's okay to get excited and have these hyper feelings you wouldn't have otherwise, so you go out and play your most spectacular game. Of course everybody thinks the other team is going to win, so you don't always have to be so careful not to make mistakes. The hard thing is to do the same against a team that's about as good as you are, or maybe just a little better. Then you're nervous. But when you're not supposed to win because the other team is the best in the state, then you can just go out there and attack. Once in a while you pull an upset. That happens about twice every three years. You do a lot more thinking and talking about an upset than you do upsetting. Usually the other team is really good and their All-State player deserves her reputation, so no matter how hard you play you still don't win. But it's fun to have an excuse to get all fired up. Of course it's not nearly so much fun when it happens the other way around. But then that's varsity.

Fremont is fifty miles away, a surprising town, and larger than you'd think it should be from the map. Fremont can also pass for a resort area in this part of the world. Cabins peek out from the woods along the river and around some old sand pits now filled with water. I sit in the stands thinking of Marian. Bo's mother and little brother are doing the same. While Jena is a sophomore, Bo is a senior; she's been to Fremont before; her mother not only knew how to find the school, but also that this is the girls' gym. I'm sitting feeling sorry for Fremont which can't afford a large fancy gym when Bo's mother starts wondering why the game isn't being played in the boys' gym. This query sets wheels to turning: Are these the tactics of playing the higher ranked? The chauvinism of not letting varsity girls play in the boys' gym on game night—whose decision was that? Have we been put here on purpose? Is there some familiarity with this home that the Fremont girls want, or know will put East at a disadvantage? How do these girls play with that concrete wall so close to the line on the other side? Are they going to push somebody into that wall? Only the last of these questions has a definite answer: yes.

Varsity is getting very physical. "Guard" means short. Guards have a lot of advantages over forwards, though. For one thing, nobody expects you to go in there and fight for rebounds, so you don't get slammed around under the basket all that much. Have you ever really watched what does on under a basket? Four or five of the biggest people on the court moving as fast as they can in a thousand different directions trying to block one another out, get crammed into a space about a fourth the size of your kitchen. It's a mess. Once in a while they get tangled up and fall down. If you're under that pile you get squashed. Then a guard goes in for the ball. It's pretty hard to actually grab a ball away from one of those big people. If you're lucky the other player will get called for traveling. If you're not lucky the guard gets called for a foul. But lots of times you get tied up and the ref calls a jump ball. Then you

*can hear the fans laughing and yelling. Forwards and centers
are about a foot taller than guards. Reserves get physical too,
but not like on varsity where everybody's bigger and faster.
That's one of the reasons they're on varsity.*

The Marian loss has the team strangled; you can see it
from the stands during warm-up. The shots that don't go
in produce more shots that don't go in, instead of the opposite—the adjustment, the smile, and the swisher. Fremont,
on the other hand, is ready, and is playing home court.
Jena calls this situation "getting homered." Bo's mother is
quiet, philosophical. Fremont is unranked, but halfway
into the second quarter is twelve points ahead. On the
other hand, being down by a dozen will do certain things
for you, relieve the pressure, loosen you up a bit, get rid of
the caution that so often comes with near victory. The
game deteriorates into raggedness and elbows. Bodies go
up, long arms claw, Fremont will have those points under
East's basket, flesh hits flesh, hard, no whistle; arms and
legs fly, but out of the mess comes Jena with the ball.

*Ice is supposed to be the environment of Eskimos, but on
varsity you get very well acquainted with ice, the miracle
drug. As a freshman in college, if you take the right courses,
you learn that Eskimos have hundreds of words for ice and
snow; they live in such close contact with the cold that it
becomes an intimate part of their lives. The same thing happens on varsity. You snuggle up to ice on your knees, elbows,
ankles—anywhere there's a hurt. You go to bed with ice. That
way you learn which brands of plastic bags leak and which
ones don't. The ice maker in your refrigerator makes cres-
cent-shaped pieces; concession stands give you shaved ice;
grocery-store ice is clear and made like cylinders. You hardly
ever see real ice cubes anymore. Motel ice machines serve up*

rectangular little blocks. You see, on varsity you can learn almost as much about ice as you can by being an Eskimo.

They materialize out of nowhere, the big ones, fast and at the favored angle aimed to intersect her at midcourt along the wall. When she drives full speed the angle is the only way, for no one can beat the laws of math and physics in a girls' gym. Up against the wall, inches from a mass of concrete block she races as only she can race, the ball pounding with a momentum that allows only one finish—layup and a crash into the pads under the basket. But they hit her at midcourt, and she hits the wall and they go down on top of her. Strain is on the floor then, the ref spins on his heels, brushes the tips of his upright fingers with the palm of his right hand, and a coach is once again in the summaries with his team. The Fremont girl chosen to carry out the execution makes both her free throws. They get the ball out of bounds and score. The gym erupts and Bo's mother has that sad sad look on her face. It's halftime, sixteen points down, fifty miles from home.

Ice seems to cure about anything as well as can be expected, at least anything important like elbows, knees, and ankles. Of course surgery helps too, but ice is the wonder drug. This is all personal opinion, not real medical expertise, but whatever works to keep you mobile on varsity, you use. Ever see someone sit with her whole foot in a bucket of ice water? That treatment takes the pain out of a sprained ankle in a hurry. Then you move your foot a little bit, stand on it, exercise the joint slowly until your leg warms up, then put it back in the bucket. Trainers, doctors, parents, friends, all have theories about how to fix joints. It usually takes about a week of icing and moving to see much improvement. If ice and gentle exercise don't work, then you have serious trouble. Ice costs next to nothing; gentle exercise is free; doctors are expensive. On varsity you get not only a course in anthropology of the Far North, but also one in the economics of pain.

The look on John Strain's face as they come back onto the court after halftime break says something has transpired in the locker room. Nobody smiles; their eyes show only the businesslike glare of having a job to do far away from home and the admission that so far they've not done it very well. Then slowly, as the third quarter ticks away, East begins to chop away at those sixteen points. Twelve, ten, eight; then Peggy hits both ends of the one-and-one and it's Fremont by six. Bo steals, she always steals; Jill rolls it in, and it's Fremont by four. In a flurry and exchange of baskets a whistle cuts through the game; East gets to within one on the three-point play, but Fremont comes back with an outside shot. The screaming is insane. You can see the sweat on their faces from the bleachers.

Varsity is having the band play for you. Band music is like no other music—especially when they play "The Championship." You're just coming out of the dressing room, standing there in the hallway next to the bleachers, Mr. Strain's getting in his last words, and about all you can see of the band is the tubas way up on the top row of their section. Little brothers play tubas. Ever see a tuba up close? They're so big, stuff like candy wrappers, milk cartons, and popcorn boxes get thrown down in there. They wrap all around a person, and sometimes right before a game you can look out and see the tubas looking back down the hall where you're waiting, and there's your brother up there with his cheeks puffed and his fingers on the valves, and he sees you and knows it's time to start playing, then those trumpets blast away and you go out on the floor dribbling, slamming it down against the boards as hard as you can, between two rows of cheerleaders. But it's the band that really gets to you . . . da da-da da da da-da . . . boom boomaboom boom . . . with the tubas laying down the rhythm and the bass drummer hitting the thing with all his might. No matter how many times you hear it, you get excited. This is your school, your court, your game and your music played by your own little brother. That's what the band means to varsity.

Ten seconds on the clock, Fremont three points ahead, Jena gets the in-bound pass beneath the basket, turns, and plunges into the full court press. And once again nobody can guard her when she explodes in rage, until a blatant personal foul sends her to the free throw line, one-and-one, three points down, two seconds to play. The gym fills with inhuman screaming, shrills of teenage girls in unison, the welling resentment of small town against the capital, the band at full force, as she begins her mental routine: The ball is bounced four times, then the elbow is placed beneath; cold blue eyes focus on the front of the rim and the first free throw hits the center of the net. The ref gathers it in and signals with his index finger the remaining shot. Strain calls time.

Varsity is worrying about your win/loss record, which of course determines whether or not you get to go to the state championship tournament; "state," it's called. You can get to state by winning your district, or if you're lucky, by a wild card invitation. Getting to state is second only to winning the tournament, or "taking state." When you're on varsity taking state is the highest goal, the dream, the finest accomplishment, the symbol of success. The best way to get named to an all-star team is to take state. Of course if you get upset a couple of times, then your wild card chances go out the window and you have to win districts, which puts a bunch more pressure on you, because districts are so unpredictable. Nobody knows why. It's just one of those things—districts are crazy tournaments. But state's a thrill. You get to play in the University's Sports Complex in front of more people than have ever watched you before. Plus you're on television. If you win, sometimes you get interviewed on TV. Being state champion tells everybody that you've accomplished everything possible on varsity. That's why at college you sometimes hear jocks saying to one another—"take state"—as they pass in the halls. It's a way of saying "remember the glory," but it's also a way of telling each other they've grown up into bigger games. You can take state all you want, but when you get to college, you're in a whole new kind of varsity.

The rasping horn shatters a gym already in crazed pandemonium, mob gone wild over red lights on a scoreboard deep in the heart of America. The roar doubles, quadruples, and Bo's mother turns to say something but while her mouth moves, bursting high school emotions are all there is to hear. But the ritual of a single free throw remains; the rules and the clock give East the dignity of an attempt which cannot, by any stretch of the imagination, succeed. Only one contest can be won now, that against total humiliation, for Fremont has the game, and knows it, and one basket becomes a test of nerves, a symbol blown all out of proportion, the last chance to tell your conquerors that there will, indeed, be another day.

Again the blue eyes get cold, again the ball is bounced four times, again the elbow goes directly underneath, and again all hell breaks loose in anger, the mob against a sixteen-year-old girl's concentration, and again the ball and net kiss. It's funny how in all that screaming you can still hear the silent sound of a perfect free throw never touching metal. It's a long drive back home from Fremont.

Varsity is sending videotapes to various colleges then waiting for a phone call. The most exciting thing is for someone to call your coach, express some interest without you writing a letter first. Then you get a tape of your best game and send it off. You wonder if math whizzes get this kind of attention, a phone call from State U. asking for a video of a kid solving an algebra problem. We look at tapes every week. Coaches always review games, tell you what you did wrong. But when that tape is going out to some college, you watch it over and over, wondering just what a coach will see. You can't edit those tapes to make you look better, like on real television. In one of our games, a tape that got sent out everywhere, I ran right into a ref's stomach. Boom; just like in a cartoon or one of those slapstick movies. A friend, in fact an obnoxiously creative, good friend, wrote this bit of script about me and the ref. It described a highly dramatic and emotional event in which a five-three guard goes slamming into the big belly of a ref. You don't do those kinds of things on purpose. Near the end of your senior year, you hope that college coaches don't wind that tape back and forth a dozen times, like this friend on varsity did, just to see you go wham into a ref's belly.

Holiday tournaments are among the most relaxed of an otherwise frenetic season. Weather permitting on the high plains, teams trek a hundred miles into the capital city, go to the museum, the art gallery, downtown shopping malls, drive through the university campus, and appear one Friday afternoon at a local high school for games sponsored by the Jaycees. Seasons are supposed to get serious in January; somehow the start of classes breathes life into rivalries, focuses attention on the rankings, potential state champions, and various colleges' recruiting targets. But on the Friday afternoon after Christmas, there's not much else to do in town but go watch a ball game, settle into the stands with a box of popcorn, and see how a tenth grader handles her first varsity tournament.

Early looks at teams you've never watched before can be educational as well as entertaining. For example, who would ever have thought Norfolk could bring to town a team as fast as horses, tall as redwoods, quick and unyielding as a stock car? Any parent who'd followed the game seriously, is who, a category into which I never fell. I simply went to watch our daughter play. Within seconds it became obvious I was not the only one getting educated. Norfolk's first round opponent is being taught basketball.

East also breezes through its first game, with one exception. In a melee under the basket she goes down. For once we're allowed into the training room. She's up on a table with a monstrous ice pack around her ankle. We've only seen the aftermath of these things before, never been so close to the event itself. She is seething, flushed, angry, breathing heavily, frustrated but never whipped. It's almost frightening to confront such adrenalin-fueled fire. She spends the rest of the game on the bench while East wins handily. She lives that night in a bucket of ice water. Norfolk, on the next day for the championship, is cold-eyed and ready. A small town plays for one thing: to beat the capital city.

College recruiting visits are eye-openers. Moms are the people to take along when you visit some school. Mothers see stuff like dorm rooms or apartments where you'll live, places to do your laundry, professors; moms are pretty hard to satisfy. Dads tend to see, or maybe imagine, the glory. But it's strange to visit any college when your old man teaches at one. You're not very surprised at what you find out; somehow growing up with a university professor takes away a lot of the mystery. It does something else, too—it makes you want to go away from home, at least a few miles. That way all your friends from high school won't be coming up to you on the street telling you what a lousy, or hard, or great, teacher your dad is, sort of depending on what they made on his last exam. On the other hand, you tend to pay attention to the academics when you sit down to dinner with one all your life. So wherever we went to look at some college, mom asked to meet with one of the professors. Some places think you're crazy to want to see a faculty member. Other places expect you to ask and have it all arranged by the time you get there. Most colleges coaches also think you're crazy when you're five-three and want to keep on playing ball.

Newspaper pictures from the holiday tournament show the Norfolk girls jumping ecstatically, as high school girls do after a tournament win. John Strain buys a bunch of these newspapers and saves them until a very cold night in February. Then he sits down alone late in his kitchen and cuts out the pictures, tapes a typed note on each one, and mails them to his team. Jena looks at the picture for a long, long time. Jubilant in the center is the Norfolk senior with whom she'd tried to do battle on an ankle that had been on ice the previous twelve hours. The regular season match with Norfolk is the next night.

Later, with the game behind her, she will collapse on the couch and savor it. East had been down by five with only a minute to go. Then came Jill's and Peggy's three-point plays and the final missed shot as the horn set off the explosion. The ankle is still intact. Norfolk became a special memory and a special word. Two years later, it would be still another Norfolk game, this time videotaped and sent upon request, that helped to answer her senior question: Is there a place that needs a guard, a special college both far and near enough from home?

One of the advantages of having a dad who teaches at a university is that once in a while you get introduced to ballplayers. Some of his former students get their pictures in Sports Illustrated. *Or, you see them on the street downtown and find out that they look different in their regular clothes. Sometimes you wouldn't be able to tell they played in college, just by their looks. We met a basketball player, Ladonna Unwin, one day out Christmas shopping. She was freezing; anybody from Florida would get cold here. Her hair was blond. She acted like she wasn't ready to take any flak off anybody. She claimed she never went to camp, but just practiced hard. She's only four inches taller than five-three. But she's on varsity, in college. Once you know someone who plays in college, and think you'd like to try it yourself, then you go watch them. Just being in that big arena, yelling for this person you met downtown, stirs up all kinds of emotions and dreams. You keep thinking—some day . . . some day . . .*

One morning in late January, acting just like I suppose millions of dads act, I ask the kid if she'd like to go watch the university women's team. Of course she answers "yes." Not too long afterward, luck produces a rare Thursday with early practice, no school assignments, and a home game. Karen declines the invitation to join us; for her, one basketball game is every basketball game unless you have a very personal interest.

In the early darkness of winter, the sports complex looms out of the deserted fairgrounds across the railroad tracks. The tracks make that hard booming sound underneath the car as stiff and frozen shock absorbers try to do their duty in the depths of the northern prairies. We have no problem finding a parking place. Admission is general. A few couples make their way through the darkness up to the feet of the enormous building. The concrete halls are almost deserted. Once inside you can choose your seats; red and the color of polished wood strike your eyes. The Lady Huskers warm up to disco music. The announcer is a man who coached a team Jena played against in the eighth grade.

For me, this building, and Ladonna Unwin, bring back scenes of a hotly political time that spelled the difference, in unforgettable fashion, between varsity at East and in the higher leagues. Once upon a time, deep in the middle of America's grain belt, a coach who'd won a national championship, the second in a row, walked into a state legislature and asked for twelve million dollars. He wanted to build a palace in which to play ball, run track, and swim. Twelve million dollars turned out not to be enough, so a year later he asked for more, and for a second time was given it. The governor, meanwhile, rose up in indignation, flexed his fiscal muscle, and lifted from the public an evidently unbearable burden—he vetoed the appropriation for a classroom building.

In this same era, three days a week, back in the back of an auditorium as decrepit as any Kansas City ghetto gym, Ladonna Unwin sat in my class fighting for her eligibility. Watching her struggle with the lecture material, my exams, and the demands of being a varsity athlete, I was continually reminded of the stark contrast between the roles of college student and basketball player. She symbolized not only the periodic conflict between these two activities, but also the kind of help society was evidently ready to give her to achieve success. She played ball in a state-of-the-art coliseum that dominated the city's northern skyline. She studied biology shoulder-to-shoulder with three hundred others in a dark room with many broken

121

seats and an unpredictable PA system. There were times I felt like yelling "Go ————!" at all those students, just like you would at some ball game.

Varsity is not wanting to quit just because it's the end of the twelfth grade. What's so magic about twelve, or about age eighteen, that it should be the end of ball? Nothing. Somewhere is a varsity that needs your help, or at the least will give you only what you ask from life itself: a chance to play. But take all the best players from all the teams you've ever faced, and put them together, and that's college. Now add a sweet upset of a major team, and a humiliating bad game against a rinky-dink school with an old high school rival. Go tell a prof you're "no dumb jock and don't intend to make a D." Get on the bus to Grand Forks and Fargo with the men's team in February, listen to rock music and basketball talk for fourteen or fifteen hours, run out of gas on the Interstate, and thank God you're a Lady Maverick guard instead of a six-ten forward guy trying to sleep in a bus seat. Get to know a radio announcer by his first name. Sign autographs for Girl Scouts. Have your stats sent to all the boosters. Get a college education. There's nothing more to ask of varsity.

We are in the general admission seats high on the south side of the Devaney Sports Complex. The women's game swings back and forth, scattered applause with every basket. Then Ladonna Unwin goes in and steals. She is small down on the floor. Jena's voice echoes through the near-empty arena, bouncing back, reverberating, a tiny voice, the kind you use at some game knowing the person will never hear but knowing also that you have to shout it out. I am totally relaxed, contemplative, absorbed in the conflicts, both political and present, that surround me, isolated, a distant observer of varsity. Jena's yelling, "Go, Donna! Go, Donna!"

14

Senior

"*H*ill Street Blues" has reached one of its more intense denouements; Karen sits staring, still in her coat, booster button still pinned to her lapel, lines of stress on her face. John III lies stretched on the sofa. On the bookcase the fish tank gurgles; its occupant, secure in the dark, drifts out of his hiding places, makes his rectangular rounds, and stares at the people grouped in the flickering light. At three minutes until ten I start my analysis of the game, but Karen turns and says she'd like to hear the last words of "Hill Street Blues" instead. Somehow the television dialogue might have accomplished something the previous three hours have not, namely, a satisfactory finish to conflict.

I say I'm sorry. John III tells his mother what was said. Jena is in the wingback, head buried in her knees. Karen takes off her coat, settles on the arm of the chair, and starts gently rubbing Jena's back. Of all the images of all the years, there could not be two more opposed than the one before me and the one I'm remembering. In my mind she sits dumped on the polished floor, smiling her most heart-melting plea, gesturing at the girl with the ball, making a tiny traveling violation sign with her index fingers at the ref who's just called her for a foul. Thirty minutes later in the darkness of her own basement she lifts her head. It has been a long time since we've seen such despair, frustration, anger, fatigue, and it's the first and only time we've seen the tears of a senior who's just lost the last home game of her high school career.

To the north is a town filled with historic names and buildings, Lutherans, money, tall and rangy workers. Beside the town is a river—wide, flat, surging in this late winter night, great curves rolling down from the mountains, a river untamed and unpredictable, fit company for a town that stands so tall and proud. Within the town lives a girl, Paula. Statuesque, vivacious, All-State, her presence on the court draws your attention; her movements, accented by her flashing golden hair, are feline; her constant smile says she knows she is all the things so many young women strive to be. While Jena sits with buried head, Paula takes her place in the courtesy line that slaps hands with losers. Her smile is indomitable; Fremont has just hammered Northeast. Tomorrow night she'll end her season, her career, at home. On Parents' Night in Fremont, she will take the floor with mom and dad, all immersed in the glory that is a graduating senior's. Then Paula will attack the court; she will press, cover the boards with panther strides, unleash a scoring burst that will burn the minds of all who watch. She will also go home after the game and share something that Jena feels now, for in less than twenty-four hours after we sit in the basement listening to the "Hill Street Blues" ending theme, Jena and Amy, two ornery little pixies, will dissect Fremont, and Paula will lose her last home game. On Parents' Night.

So down it's come to this.

It must be time to back away, ask what's happened, see where we've gone and what's been won and lost.

Some teachers have learned and taught things they never expected to. John Strain's acquired a certain calmness; he'll never again give anyone the pleasure of his technicals. Instead, he'll take the loss, stoically, if it comes. But late at night in your living room he'll talk of books he's read, tell you how they say it's all right to win, and make you feel he's trying to justify the competitiveness he barely keeps under control. Funny, you never think about coaches reading books. But he's one of only two teachers in twelve years who've given a book to a little girl, a book that tells her to be everything and anything she wants, to think and dig deep for that person inside who can beat all the odds against success on any court, symbolic or otherwise. He's tried to teach plays, but he's taught instead a brand of brutal and naïve honesty that starts a kid, and plays a kid, and never lets one linger on the bench for long who can handle spheres or rise to challenges. He's also learned to spend a time-out to ask an out-of-town ref not to tell Julie "now watch your feet; don't step over the line" every time he hands her the ball for a free throw, unless he tells the hometown girls the same thing, which he doesn't. And in the morning, Jena inhales orange juice, wastes no sad thoughts over the Fremont seniors' loss on Parents' Night, and tells us in the space between her words that with all the miles, nights on Blue Bird buses, Eagles music, popcorn, pizza, Diet Pepsi, laughs, trophies, ice or rain and the pounding of a basketball, we've still not scratched the surface of this game. For in a city by a river, a ref can still tell a girl to watch her toes on the free throw, and two running, stealing, passing, dribbling leprechauns can help deliver the home team to a visiting coach's feet on a silver platter. Thanks, Mr. Strain; it's been great.

And Larry watches Amy, on the floor with Jena, and suddenly the Angels' time is gone, funny how it came so quickly after all those never-ending years; there'll be no Kansas City now, no Milford, Hampton, Ramada Inn, rooms around the swimming pool, parents talking late of moves among the lines and circles, and how it seemed the only thing to do, to simply sit on wooden seats and watch the girls play ball. Life was so uncomplicated when they were ten, when the league was City Rec, not high school, and everybody played for fun instead of championships. Yet one person's decision, Larry's moment in history, opened the doors for a child. A running back cannot graduate from college, yet he is somehow "worth" four million dollars. A college coach comes off a banner year, the season ticket sales explode, but then he plays the next season to empty houses because he does not win. But a man who works for IBM, and played a generation back at a college oh so small, can just decide he'd like to coach a team and suddenly the air's alive. You cannot teach a child forever, Larry knows, nor can you see ahead to games that wait for Angels on their many courts.

Except that no one took the childhood sport too seriously, at first; there was only pure instruction, the quiet voice and clatter of a backboard in a church's gym where once the Reverend sat down to coffee at sunrise Easter breakfast on the free throw line. Then Peggy got a scholarship. An Angels forward, always smiling, easygoing, cool, open for the corner shot, slapping hands with teammates at the score, she packed her bags for college. We turned to look again. Games were not what we thought. We laughed when Jena stole the basketball, and Amy did her jumping jacks, cold-eyed, and when they lost the sadness didn't last for long. Then came Peggy's scholarship. We saw at last what ball had taught: To hate to lose so much and want to win so much you'll work so hard you'll never lose again; but when you do you'll calmly eat your innards out and watch the trophy that you've never touched go into another's locker room. The trophy's gone, but no one will ever take your sense of what it means to earn your dreams. Don't rest, player, for down the road lie other games in higher leagues where things come as hard and fast as Jena's half-court pass. The childhood times are gone, Larry, over. Thanks, coach; it's been magnificent.

What's been won? To answer, turn to math where transformations are commonplace, analogies are stretched, and one is carried into fields where nested concepts fold in more and more experience, explaining everything. The abstract algebra of games has rules for handling variables, adding some, subtracting others, multiplying, dividing, placing them into relationships with equal signs until an answer, suddenly, shines at the bottom of the page. Scholars often have a certain arrogance because they see so few distinctions in the patterns that our lives display. Those familiar equations can be recognized in organizations, crowds and places that have nothing to do with sport.

At the beginning, we had a problem: Child plus "x," multiplied many times over, equals a being whose experience of having walked the face of earth will be on the one hand unique, yet on the other shared with all humanity, living, past, and to come. The unknown quantity, "x," can itself be an equation, a combination of constants and variables. Somehow as parent we must solve for "x," or else wonder forever about our offspring's singular place in all the panoramic interactions, realized and potential, implied in that word: human. At the end, we saw a solution— "x" equalled ball plus coach plus game. We've won a look at what defines our species: teaching; the development of potential into reality.

One year back so far in time a nameless high school

coach stood and watched the naked boys go race a clock. Chlorine touched your molecules and sent its stinging breath into your brain so even now one whiff and back you go, up and down, bleached hair and earaches, eyes that stare back red. Once a teacher stood, with a clock in hand, then another, and another, and some were good and some were bad. A generation later we ask what made them so. The answer is simple: For the good ones you went fast, for the bad ones, slow. Fast good; slow bad. We are not happy with such simple answers now. Why? What did they do, the good ones? What they did is teach.

They taught a child to swim, to reach for all there is, to want to find the limits, to have no fear of standing on a box a mile of laps away from rest and crave the gun that barks "go test yourself!" That's what the good ones taught. They showed us what to learn, and how to learn, by their tone of voice, posture, a sense of values placed correctly. In retrospect, the complexity of our kind is shown to us upon the fields of friendly strife. We ask what it is to be human, to have spent some time on earth, a question no beetle ever knew. At the end we know: We've been taught, the thing a human does so well no other can come close. To teach, to learn, to teach to learn and learn to teach—that's what there is to life beyond the work, the sleeping and eating, the predators and prey. Thanks, coach, it's been wonderful.

And what's been lost? A feeling of simplicity, comfort, the luxury of a childhood fantasy that sometimes even an older person uses to build an image, a castle, a frame to hold the life events. If she has such a structure in the years ahead, it won't be made of hoops or nets, and may not be a game at all. Her world will speak to her electronically sometimes; she'll always pause and watch another dance upon some court or turf, in far-off places, on a phosphorescent screen whose shadows splash reflected on her face until she tires of moves she's seen a thousand times and turns the television off. To have played is to have learned the truth: No matter what an announcer says, sport's not Eden, it's effort and pain, a joy so deep at having used your best and won; it's a place to be a human, not a god, to taste the salt, to say goodbye to prisons of those dreams of victory without the labor. She'll never sit and think herself into a championship with grand naïveté.

A fear is also lost, gone with bitter shots in final seconds, overtimes, mysterious fourth quarters, parents that you used to like before their daughters beat the Blue and White. The fear of failure keeps so many thoughts inside a head, so many men and women in their chairs, silent, acceding, not wanting to be thought a fool, or stand out, or gather social species' hate for doing well, or poorly, or any other way but average. How much raw intelligence, ability, vision, lies fallow in such fear? A world and then a world, is how much. Such a load to place on ball. But fear is fear and what's lost is gone, no matter what it is. If you want them badly enough to drain your mind and soul in front of screaming mobs and pounding drums, the points become all things lost through the ages: Pride, love, hope, and most importantly, the fear of failure itself.

Newspapers print the facts one day, light a fireplace the next, and with them goes the record of how we played. The sun still comes up. My dog was still glad to see me in the morning. My French teacher still spoke a foreign language; math grades didn't change; my car started; sparrows flittered in the sleeping winter roses as they always have. So what's been lost? A game. I've done it once and lived. So what's so bad about a loss? There are some things I cannot do. One person does not make a team. No, but one person does not sit and watch in silent fear while the world slips away. Instead, you crave the chance to catch it quickly, want the action, want the victory enough to put your heart on court for all to see. So what's been lost? The fear that stifles effort. I tried my best and then some more and that's the key.

I have an image in my mind, of a young person, standing on the edge of town. The highway stretches to a flat line between the land and sky. The child bends the horizon into various shapes, testing them against her vision of herself. All match; she can be anything, or everything. Beneath her left arm is a basketball. As she starts down the highway, that special flip of the wrist sends the ball pounding against the concrete. The sound fades as she walks out into the world.